# What people say abo.. ...... .......

'Simon is at the forefront of thinking in business. His revolutionary operational process for his team is an example of why he gained an Investors in People Gold award. Simon really cares and goes to the nth degree to deliver fantastic customer service. Any business which needs help must have a meeting with Simon.'

*— Rob Walsh, Owner and Managing Director,*
*Clear Vision Accountancy Group*

'I've spoken at and attended literally thousands of conferences. No one has inspired me like Simon. Get this – he's an accountant! But he's clearly a great leader, he runs a truly awesome business, he inspires his clients to do great things and no one I've ever seen reaches out and grabs an audience the way Simon does. Ideas flow from him at an amazing rate – and they're not just ideas but literally things that Simon does in his business. That's the really cool part. Get to know Simon either through his book (it's great too), his speeches, or indeed by becoming a client. Whichever one (or ones!) you choose, it'll be one of the smartest business decisions you've ever made.'

*— Paul Dunn, Chairman, BUY1GIVE1*

'I've known Simon for a little over 18 months. During that time, Simon has been a source of inspiration on how an innovative firm should be run. Recently I listened to Simon speak on his business development ideas, in particular his passion, BRAVEST Business. As always, I found him truly inspiring and challenging to the norms of the profession.'

*— Stuart Ramsay, Owner,*
*Accountancy Extra*

'I spent an interesting and stimulating two days at a summit where Simon was one of five guest speakers. I learnt how he provides excellent service to his customers, involves his team, and how to transform our own business. His ideas force you to challenge your more conventional thinking and practices – he's truly inspirational and I would recommend using him to anyone that wants to truly change their business.'

*– Tony Kensington, Aspirations Accountancy*

# Banish the Bottleneck

7 savvy steps to grow the (almost) perfect team for your accountancy practice

SIMON CHAPLIN

# Contents

# Free Gifts!

As a thank you for reading this book, I'd like to give you a set of free gifts:

- A simple team member survey you can use to gather team member views before your Away Day.

- The BSOCK and PSOCK Excel template I used to record the KPIs at GreenStones.

- A Skills Matrix to help you grow your team into customer managers so they can look after them brilliantly.

- A video called 'How to use the Skills Matrix in your practice' so you can start delegating those tasks and developing your team now.

- A working template of a 'Letter of Expectation' so you can see how to get absolute clarity on outputs for an underperforming team member.

- And lastly, you'll get a PDF of the GreenStones 'money' I talk about in the 'Make It a Game' section of this book so you can use it as a template to motivate your team.

Here's the link:

www.BanishTheBottleneck.com/FreeGiftsFromSimon

...or simply scan this QR code with the camera on your phone.

# About the Author

Simon Chaplin has been running his award-winning accountancy practice since 2002. He has figured out what it takes to have an (almost) perfect team and has also won several awards, including Employer of the Year at the British Accountancy Awards.

In this book, he guides you through the whole process of getting from an unproductive and unengaged team to a productive, high-performing team you can be proud of.

He was diagnosed with dyslexia (aged eight) and, as a result, his headmaster told him, 'Nothing good will ever come of you.' Simon set about proving him wrong. Having never been academically gifted, Simon stumbled into the accountancy profession in 1992 and found he had a knack for it.

Three years after becoming one of the youngest people in the UK to hold both a chartered accounting and tax qualification, Simon bought an accountancy practice called GreenStones at the age of 27.

In the first three years of owning the practice, Simon and his team doubled the number of team members, tripled the turnover and quadrupled the profits of the business. He did all that while training for the London Marathon (raising more than £10,000 for the Arthritis Research Campaign), qualifying as a hypnotherapist, and cycling 963 miles from Land's End to John O'Groats.

GreenStones achieved Investors in People Gold at the first attempt (only 1% of IIP businesses do this), attained Customer First Status, as well as winning numerous other awards including National Firm of the Year.

Having extracted himself from the day-to-day running of GreenStones, Simon now spends his time inspiring, challenging and supporting accountants and their teams to be the best they want to be.

Through his consultancy business, The Accountants' Mastermind, he is a highly regarded author, speaker and consultant. Simon's down-to-earth, real-life approach to teaching through the use of stories is compelling and gives you the opportunity to be the best you can be.

# Introduction

This book is for accountancy practice leaders who are getting in the way of their own business's growth.

I have been there.

I want to share with you how I learnt to delegate – not just on one-off tasks, but *in a thorough, systematised way that impacts everything about the way we do business.*

Do any of these statements resonate with you?

- I'm the first to arrive in the office and the last to leave.
- I live under the tyranny of the urgent and don't make time for long-range planning.
- I run around after customers to make sure they are being looked after (often not getting paid for the extra work).
- I often find myself getting frustrated with my team, spotting simple errors and then having to tell them off.
- I constantly find myself double-checking my team's work.
- My team don't seem to understand what we're doing or why.
- I spend all weekend catching up with the work my team didn't get done during the week.
- I work far too many hours trying to please all of my customers, and it is costing me my health and time with my family.
- I want to grow my practice but I'm scared to take on more team members. If I do, there's the risk they'll perform the

same way as my current team.

- I've read loads of books and listened to many podcasts, but what I really need is for someone to *tell me what to do!*

- I'd love to be able to help my team develop and improve, but my firm doesn't have the money for expensive courses.

I've just painted a picture of my own life in 2009. I owned my own accountancy practice, GreenStones, but I was working too hard. I was the *bottleneck* in my practice.

It was a bit like when putting roadworks on a motorway. The motorway narrows to a bottleneck, the cars slow, and before long the traffic has backed up for miles!

I was the roadworks. If I delegated poorly, forgot to train the team in a specific aspect or simply believed that I was 'the best person for the job', then the practice would slowly grind to a halt.

I created the bottleneck with the very best of intentions! I wanted to ensure that everything our practice produced was faultless – and I believed that I was the only one who could make that happen.

This never-ending desire to make sure our customers were always taken care of gave me the perfect excuse to eat rubbish, smoke, and drink wine – either to celebrate, commiserate or relax.

Hopefully, I've got to you before you reach the extremes that I was facing! But if any of this sounds like the road you are on, this book is for you.

Here's what my life looks like now:

- I have a wonderful team of 22 who do a sterling job of

inspiring, challenging and supporting our customers.

- I don't micromanage my team members because I trust them with the day-to-day running of the business.

- The team have the freedom to work where and when they like as long as they produce the work we agree should be completed.

- My practice has systems in place that enable the team to deliver an excellent service to our customers without me needing to be involved. The team know exactly what to do and when to do it.

- I am not afraid of a customer deciding to stop working with us because of something I said or a challenge I made.

- I can work from a position of what's right for the customer, not to protect myself.

At this point, GreenStones turns over £1.4m, and my fee base is £23,000 of that.

I'm still involved in the practice but, more often than not, I just attend the monthly board meetings, and pop in if there's a team challenge or the senior team needs some support. I don't measure it, but I'd say it works out roughly one day a week on average.

This allows me to spend a large amount of time with my wife Sally and my children Ben and Aimie, run The Accountants' Mastermind and go hiking once in a while. I take most of the school holidays off and have never missed a sports day or a nativity play.

The profits from my business enable me to live a lifestyle I only dreamed of as a child, coach freely, invest in other businesses and make a contribution to the charities I support.

Throughout this book you will learn the steps I believe you need to take to get the team you have always wanted.

## How Do You Get There?

The greatest paradigm shift that I need you to make is to stop thinking about inputs – how much you're doing and how you're doing it; and start thinking about outputs – the *results* that you and your team are getting.

Here's what that looks like. We operate under a set of well-defined KPIs for the practice which are broken down into team member KPIs. Each team member is required to meet their numbers by the end of the month. If this happens, the practice as a whole meets its targets.

My team operate under a system of 'flexible work'. That means that they can choose to work from the office or from their homes or from their boats! It doesn't matter to me what hours they work as long as they are also available when customers need them.

The process I use to get practices to this point is called SOCKSUP. My late mother, Christine, used to tell me, 'Pull your socks up, Simon,' so it seemed a fitting name to use when I started coaching.

Once you've completed this process, your practice will effectively run without you if you want it to. Your confident, competent team will know exactly what to do and when to do it. You will have the choice to be at work if you want or be way from the office doing the things you enjoy.

As you can imagine, working in this manner requires you to have a great deal of trust in your team – we'll talk later about how to get there.

Periodically, you'll find suggested action steps to help you along the way. However, this book is not a blueprint, playbook or bible for you to implement. It worked for us and has worked (with tweaks) for the many accountants I have worked with through The Accountants' Mastermind. Our stories should be an inspiration, a challenge and a support through the process – an idea generator if you stumble on your particular journey.

# SET THE SCENE
# OUTLINE THE PLAN
# CONFIRM AND CONVERSE WITH THE TEAM
# KNOW WHAT TO GET OFF YOUR PLATE
# SET THE PERSONAL KPIs
# UNITE AROUND PROGRESS
# PROJECT FORWARD

*The SOCKSUP process*

## How to Use This Book

If you're not ready to take all the SOCKSUP steps laid out in the book, that's okay. Sprinkled throughout the book you'll find Quick Wins that you can take right away. Pick some or all of them, but I think you'll see a high return on investment when you do!

As you read through this book, scribble comments, thoughts

and possible actions in the gaps and spaces between sections and chapters. Once you've added your thoughts and actions, you can type up a plan to implement with your team.

I've also included a series of questions to provoke your thinking.

To inspire, challenge and support you to improve on what we have achieved at GreenStones.

Often, the answers will pop straight into your head. That's great. Make sure you write them down before they disappear again. If you don't, the memory (and the emotion you had with it) will fade.

> *This never-ending desire to make sure our customers were always taken care of gave me the perfect excuse to eat rubbish, smoke, and drink wine – either to celebrate, commiserate or relax.*

If answers don't pop up, let the question settle. Think about the issue in the shower, on your run or when you are doing the washing up. Meditate on it if you are that way inclined. Play with it. Eventually, an answer will come to mind. If not, don't fret.

Just know this...

Whatever you decide to do with this book, don't beat yourself up if you don't take as much action as you'd like. Just accept it. You will get there in the end.

I'm here cheering you on all the way, cheering, celebrating your wins and encouraging you to be the best you want to be. If you need any support or any further clarity, please reach out. My contact details are towards the end of the book.

As I always say, I like stupid questions. Stupid questions are easy to answer. So please feel free to ask one if you think you have one.

Whatever you do, don't use the possibility of looking stupid or daft as an excuse to stand still.

I now invite you to delve in with an open mind, have fun, laugh at me (and yourself) occasionally, but most of all, take action. Without action, nothing will change.

## A Note About Words

As you read, you'll notice that I use the term 'customer' rather than 'client' when referring to the very kind people who pay our salaries.

For me, 'client' implies that the company has ownership over the relationship. It also suggests an ongoing relationship, which might relax the team into thinking the customers will come back week after week, month after month, and year after year. At GreenStones, we use 'customer' as this allows the team to think seriously about each transaction. We must make sure that our customers stay customers.

Your company may continue to use the word 'client', many still do! Choose what suits your values and culture.

> **Without action, nothing will change.**

I also use the term 'team member' rather than 'staff' or 'employee'.

It sends a shiver down my spine every time I hear someone use the word 'staff'! To me, it conjures up images of a stately home somewhere in the rolling hills with a lord or lady still in charge, longing for Queen Victoria to be on the throne.

'Employee' is only slightly better – it still creates a divide, a lack of connection. 'Employee and employer'. What advantage is that to you other than massaging your ego or helping you have a sense of authority?

'Team member' or 'colleague' is much more inclusive and equal. I use 'team member' throughout this book. Again, I encourage you to think about the connotation of the words you use and choose what best suits your company.

# STEP 1
## SET THE SCENE

# Step 1 – Set the Scene

Step 1 is all about you, your team and your workplace culture. It begins with describing how you function now, and it ends with a bold suggestion for revolutionising your team culture. You'll begin to focus on the results your team gets instead of on micromanaging how they get them! This is a crucial step towards removing yourself as the practice's bottleneck.

## Who Are Your Team?

Your team are the backbone of your practice. Without your team and their support, you are banging your head against a brick wall.

You may be proud of what you achieve together. They may be friends, long-time acquaintances or even family.

But something's missing – a spark, a fire in the belly to take them to the next level.

And here's where the problem lies: *a lack of direction.*

They're going through the motions. They turn up, do the job (just enough to stay on your good side) and then disappear bang on time to carry on with their lives – leaving you to do what they have not done.

*It doesn't have to be this way.*

The goal is to create volunteers – team members who are so good they could work for any competitor for the same salary they are on now... but still choose to work for your practice because of how good you are.

Remember that your team members have far more uncertainty in their working lives than you do because *you* are the one who knows what the company is doing. It doesn't matter how much you show them and talk to them and support them – they will never know as much as you do about where the practice is going and what you're planning to do.

But, they trust in your abilities as a leader. They trust you to look after them. They trust you to pay their salaries at the end of the month. Make sure you trust them too.

 Download the free resource at
WWW.BANISHTHEBOTTLENECK.COM/FREEGIFTSFROMSIMON
to grade your team on 'Know, Like and Trust'.

Having team members that you know and like is important, but having team members you trust is vital! Have a play with the above Know, Like and Trust exercise – it takes less than 30 seconds per team member, and you might learn something about your relationships!

## Five Steps to Developing Your Team

In his book, *The Five Dysfunctions of a Team*, Patrick Lencioni shares the five disciplines you need to develop the team you want for your practice. They are:

- Trust
- Conflict

- Commitment
- Accountability
- Results.

Each stage is dependent on the previous stage, but ultimately, none can ever be 'finished'. All relationships can move up and down the stages, too, depending on how you are interacting at any one time.

Here's my take on them and how they have affected my time at GreenStones...

## Trust

Every relationship you have – with your partner, your children, your sports team, or your team at work – is formed on trust.

The higher that level of trust, the better your team will function. If you don't have trust, you can't have proactive conflict.

You might like to revisit the 'Know, Like and Trust' resource I shared in the previous section and see how you scored each team member on trust. Ask yourself why you gave them that score. Did they do something in the past to upset you? Do you have unresolved conflict with them that needs addressing – or is it beyond repair?

An important component of trust is vulnerability. I'd like to share a personal story about how I learnt to be vulnerable with my team and how that impacted our company culture.

### The Big Swimming Pool Lie

I felt ashamed. I'd lied. I felt stupid driving home from work that day.

And I knew I had to do something about it. Something that

made me uncomfortable. Something that helped me deal with the inner demons that were holding me back.

It was 2008. I was 35. My wife Sally and I were in the process of buying our dream house. It was a huge stretch for us – both financially and mentally.

As you'd expect, I'd worked on the budgets, and I knew that we'd be okay financially if the practice continued to develop and grow.

But it was scary. I'd had a modest upbringing and never dreamt I'd own a house with a swimming pool!

The team knew I was buying a house, but I hadn't elaborated on what it was like.

Then one of my team members asked (in front of everyone), 'Does your new house really have a swimming pool?'

Without thinking or hesitation, I said, 'No,' and quickly changed the subject.

I never intended to lie about it. The surprise of being asked, plus the fear around what the team would think of me, knocked me off balance.

On the drive home, I gave a lot of thought to why I'd lied. I was embarrassed about our success. I'd sought the team's (and my wider network's) approval for what we were doing. I didn't want anyone to think I had gotten 'above my station' and was fleecing the business.

But if I wasn't comfortable earning money and being rewarded for my actions, how on earth could I help my team and customers get comfortable with being successful?

I resolved to make a change.

And the first step was being brave enough to admit the lie and share how I felt about it.

At the next opportunity, I had one of the most difficult conversations I have had as an owner of an accountancy practice.

In front of the whole team, I explained that I hadn't answered the 'swimming pool' question honestly. I admitted that the new house did have a swimming pool, and five acres of garden too.

I shared why I'd lied when I was first asked and how that had made me feel. I then apologised to the team for letting each of them down.

The energy in the room was almost tangible. Something shifted. My shortcomings and insecurities had taken the team connection to the next level.

I'd been brave. I felt like a leader.

The swimming pool story still gets talked about in the office occasionally... mostly at my expense!

> **My shortcomings and insecurities had taken the team connection to the next level.**

However, sharing stories is an excellent way for the values to be passed on to new team members. It helps them learn about the values of GreenStones less formally. They are far more likely to remember the story (and what it meant) than a word or a phrase they cannot connect with.

I've learnt a lot about myself since that day. I still have hang-ups like everyone else, but I am much more comfortable talking about money and the challenges around having money or not having money. Some might say I have gone too far as I now freely share the practice results, and every team member has access to my personal tax return on the office computer system.

When you think about what you share with your team, ask yourself:

'What am I hiding that is holding the team and me back? Is there something I could share that would help them make better decisions?' In a later chapter, I'll be challenging you to share financial information with your team. *How* do you feel about that? *What* makes you feel that?

How much better could you and your team be if you let go of any hang-ups and delivered a service free from constraints? How much better could you serve your customers? How much better would you feel inside?

Take the step. Share more. Choose to be more vulnerable with your team. I guarantee you won't regret it.

## Conflict

Why do partners in long-term relationships have so many arguments? Aside from the fact that no one likes to do the washing up, partners can fight because they trust each other. They can share their feelings and be vulnerable without fear of the consequences. If you don't have trust, you won't say what you really think, and resentment begins to boil beneath the surface. But once you have trust, conflict can be productive: you can work out a compromise about the washing up, and you can commit to the decision that came out of the conflict.

Many of us fear conflict, but robust, healthy conflict is a sign of a functional relationship. Wouldn't it be great if your team trusted you enough to have healthy conflict?

Team members who don't feel safe enough to have conflict

won't share their concerns within the conversation you are having. They won't feel heard. This means that, ultimately, they won't be committed to the decision that is made.

Instead, they nod politely and then moan to their colleagues, friends and anyone else that will listen about why the decision is a bad one and will never work.

> *Robust, healthy conflict is a sign of a functional relationship.*

That's not an engaged team member working with you to achieve your practice's goals. As you know, business leaders do not have a monopoly on great ideas. It might be a little bit scary listening to how your idea can be improved but, ultimately, it is always in the best interests of your practice.

Once team members feel trusted, we can encourage them to share their opinions firmly and respectfully.

## Commitment

When you have high trust and productive conflict (and it's a never-ending process), you start to build commitment. If your team members feel like they have been heard and their opinions are taken into consideration, they are more likely to commit to a decision you make. It's because they fully understand the rationale behind the decision.

*Quick Win*: Make the commitment overt and have absolute clarity about:

- what will be done
- who will do it
- when it will be done

- what resources are necessary and how to procure them

- what might prevent the course of action from being completed.

Ideally, the actions will be written down and circulated across the team. They must be shared with everyone who is involved in implementing the decision.

## Accountability

The team members trust each other and you. They have freely debated and challenged any decision that has been made. They have committed to the decision and the actions they need to take as a result.

You only need to focus on accountability if you are not getting the results you want and you feel you have already done solid work on the first three steps.

In a nutshell, what I mean by 'accountability' is task oversight: making sure that team members follow through on the steps they've agreed to.

Team members can be held accountable by:

- themselves,

- their teammates, and

- you.

In a perfect world, team members should hold themselves accountable because they believe in the work they're doing. If that's not happening, you have a challenge. Maybe the team member has other challenges going on in their lives that are taking precedence at the moment. You need to find out. Could you support them and take action?

If a team member is not self-motivated, perhaps they will feel motivated by their sense of duty to the team.

Everyone should respect and trust their teammates. That means performing at the top of their game to help their teammates achieve what they have set out to do.

When you have the first three steps working (trust, commitment and accountability), this becomes the default position. The team member will feel embarrassed in front of the others if they haven't performed as well as they said they would.

For some people, this team accountability is what drives them more than anything else.

If neither self-motivation nor team motivation is working, there are two problems I often see that lead to the practice owner needing to hold everyone else accountable.

> *If a team member is not self-motivated, perhaps they will feel motivated by their sense of duty to the team.*

One is a lack of clarity from the practice owner. The team member doesn't know what is required of them. If they don't know, and you don't know, how on earth are they going to achieve the result you want!

Another possibility is that the team have got used to you taking work from them. This is an easy trap to fall into, as it often feels more manageable in the moment. Has your ego got in the way? Is there a lack of trust? Are you protecting a team member?

If there are no extenuating circumstances, and the team member simply can't be bothered to be accountable (even when they know how important it is to you and the team), it might be time to wave goodbye. Ensure you are clear that you have done all that you can before you take this drastic step! (We'll talk more about how to do that in Step 5, Set the Team Member KPIs.)

### *Accountability is Subjective, Not Objective!*

Holding people accountable is not an exact science. When I first started on this process, I hoped – believed – the solution to all my challenges was holding team members accountable based on objectives, prescribed numbers, and goals. At the end of the month or quarter, I wanted to look at a set of numbers and decide if action needed to be taken. But I couldn't. There still had to be a subjective decision process on whether to move someone on to or up the disciplinary process. There is still a managerial decision to be made if a team member is not performing: Does the team member stay or go?

I still struggle with this dilemma now and again because I don't like having difficult conversations.

Some say I hang on to underperforming team members for too long. But I point to success stories where team members struggled at first but, over time, turned into star players.

You never know for sure what makes the change, but I believe that it helps when you, the team member and the team all know exactly where they stand.

In situations where you need to hold a team member accountable, I use the HEFFF process I'll share later in the book.

## Results

Recognising results is a bit difficult sometimes. People are keen to move on. Yes, the job's done, we did it, what's next?

How do you celebrate your successes? Do you feel

uncomfortable sharing them? Do you feel unworthy of being successful? What stops you from celebrating? (This is a great topic for the Away Day as we'll discuss later.)

You might have implemented a new piece of software, won a new customer, saved a customer loads of tax. I bet there are more than you think!

Whether your results for a given project are what you hoped or not, you still have work to do.

Let's say you get good results. Celebrate! Reward the whole team. It can be anything from a simple, conscious thank you to a team holiday in the Bahamas.

**Quick Win:** Work out what makes your team and team members feel appreciated, and next time you have a big team win, go for it! That might mean public or private recognition, a medal or a chocolate bar.

> *For some people, team accountability is what drives them more than anything else.*

Now let's say you get poor results. If things aren't going your way, you need to beat yourself up, right? You need to have a drink and eat a giant Dairy Milk bar, right?

It doesn't have to be that way.

**Quick Win**: Reflect, debrief and commit for next time so you don't make the same mistakes again.

My favourite way to debrief is to ask two simple questions:

- What went well with this project?
- What would have made it even better?

They are called **What Went Well (WWW)** and **Even Better If (EBI)**. If you have a good foundation of trust, you'll get good responses from these questions.

Once you have your answers, review them and decide what action you'll take to improve results in the future.

Without completely ignoring the negatives, focus on the good stuff that is happening. No one likes being around a moaning Minnie for any length of time.

It's better to build than it is to knock down.

## Prepare to Be Let Down

Your friends, family and sports club members have let you down from time to time, haven't they? Undoubtedly, the same will happen at work. And the more trust you have extended towards your team, the worse the breach of trust can be.

*At some point a team member will let you down.*

They'll ring in sick when they are not, pinch the petty cash, or embarrass themselves at the Christmas party. There are an infinite number of ways they can let you and themselves down.

However, you're in control of how you respond to that situation. You can get bitter, moan a lot, and vow never to recruit another team member.

And as for team members you've still got, what should you do? Create rules and procedures to stop them from doing anything you think they shouldn't? This might (or might not) make a troublesome 5% of team members stay in line, but I guarantee it will upset the other 95%. That's how you end up with a 94-page handbook that no one reads!

Don't allow those who let you down to affect your relationship with everybody else.

Instead, be very conscious of the rules you make to ensure that you're not destroying trust. As you've seen, if trust within your practice goes down, then you *won't* have productive conflict. Instead, you'll have a lack of commitment, little to no accountability and unsatisfactory results.

Let me tell you about a time I was let down by a team member.

Many years ago, before I allowed the team to work where and when they wanted, I caught a team member (let's call her Susan) selling jewellery at a car boot sale on a day she'd rang in sick!

I'd been tipped off by another team member who thought it was unfair to the rest of the team and to me. I knew if I'd confronted Susan about what she was doing, she'd have just denied it. I needed to get proof.

I doubted myself on the way over to the car boot sale, beating myself up for not trusting Susan. I was secretly hoping that it wouldn't be true. I'd got a big speech planned, inspired by Alan Sugar on *The Apprentice*, if it was.

I was getting more and more nervous as I drew into the car park. I was kind of like a private detective but hoping not to solve the 'case'.

Then I saw Susan. And Susan saw me. We made eye contact.

Instead of the confident, 'you're fired' speech I'd planned to give, I said nothing. I just turned away and walked back to the car. I felt sad and let down. I'm pleased I didn't confront her there and then. I'd have probably said something I'd have regretted later. I have no idea what Susan did – she probably carried on selling the jewellery!

Needless to say, that team member didn't last long after that.

Now, I could've let that experience influence my sick pay policy and make me doubt every team member whenever they called in sick. It might even have had me riding around car boot sales each week looking for profiteering team members!

But I didn't let that happen. After I calmed down, it didn't change my relationship with the 95% of team members who follow the rules and want the best for me, the customers and the practice.

You have the same choice each time someone lets you down. You can create systems, processes and rules to stop it from happening again, but these are very rarely successful and, more likely than not, will upset the team members that didn't get it wrong.

It's much better to forgive the person, chalk it up to experience and move on.

## Relax the Hold on Your Team

Rather than becoming hypervigilant about possible wrongdoers, I recommend showing trust in your team by giving them more latitude, not less. If your team are getting their work done effectively, why micromanage where, when and how they do their work?

I recommend a 'work anywhere' policy that allows your team members to work where they like, when they like and how they like. ('Even on the beach?!' asked one team member. Yes, even on the beach!) Once again, this puts the focus on the results they are getting – their outputs – rather than the minutiae of how they got there – their inputs.

## What Will the Team Think?

Your team is likely to have a wide range of reactions at the start. I think the best way for me to tell you about that is in the words of some of my team members.

For some, it took a while to adjust to the change:

- 'I found it quite a challenge mentally to allow myself to go from the traditional 9-to-5 to being able to choose when and where I worked, but I got used to it. Now I manage my own time and work when it's best for me.' – *Leigh Barraclough*

- 'This was totally alien and seemed unworkable for someone who stuck religiously to the standard 9-to-5 concept. I was, at best, sceptical… It wasn't until I received a phone call one morning in the office that I first realised the full benefits of this system. I had to leave immediately as a family member had been taken ill, and without hesitation, I was out of the door within minutes.' – *Michael Weatherington*

Some reported that the change wasn't as big a deal as they expected:

- 'I still came to work at the same time, did my hours and went home.' – *Michael Weatherington*

- 'In the first few months of flexible working being an option, I pretty much stuck to my usual 8.30am to 4.30pm routine in the office as I enjoyed being around my colleagues.' – *Jordan Farrance*

- 'I still enjoy laughs with colleagues [from home]. One colleague in particular calls me quite regularly!' – *Dani Wragg-Long*

35

Of course, any major culture shift will come with its drawbacks:

- 'The worst thing is that the team spirit which was there before has somewhat diminished.' – *Leigh Barraclough*

- 'You do feel obliged to reply to emails whatever time of day they are received, and with it being a target-driven process this does lend itself to a more individual or selfish working environment. At the start, certain people would prolong or rush through accounts jobs depending on the next job's quality. I work more hours a week now than I ever did doing the standard working week but, in my opinion, it's worth the flexibility.' – *Michael Weatherington*

But overall, the team reported benefits both to themselves and to the practice:

- 'You feel trusted, empowered and responsible.' – *Nicola Hawksley*

- 'It was really useful to be able to stay at home and work if I wasn't feeling up to coming into the office, or to be able to leave in the middle of the day, without explanation, if I was needed somewhere by a family member.' – *Jordan Farrance*

- 'From being at home for that special delivery you cannot miss to attending your child's Christmas concert without worrying about making up the time, it can be a real asset.' – *Michael Weatherington*

- 'The amount of money and time I have saved by working from home is unbelievable, I get up at 7.30 am without needing to rush around and stress myself out, have some breakfast, tidy my house and then begin work. I feel as though I want to give back more to a company that puts so much trust in me.' – *Dani Wragg-Long*

- 'When we made the change, it felt like we were free from the restrictions and stresses of structured working. Simon trusted us to manage our time more effectively, which produced more motivation and commitment to GreenStones.' – *Beverly Green*

- 'It makes you happier overall and just makes good sense. When you spread your workload out, it doesn't feel like working all the time. You tend to not clock-watch, and concentrate on the task at hand. While working, you start focusing on adding value, prioritising key tasks, getting work done and not just being present.' – *Mark Wrigley*

- 'I work part-time (mainly from home) at GreenStones and feel it gives me the opportunity to work when I'm fully engaged and around my family life rather than when I have other things on my mind. I have the freedom to attend school events and doctor's appointments without feeling like I have to negotiate time off or justify myself to anyone.' – *Sally Wrigley*

Some of your team will be excited; many will be nervous. It may be out of their comfort zone. Their friends and family, through lack of understanding, might also add to that anxiety. It will be very different to anything they have experienced, and they may think there's an ulterior motive! One or two of your team might not like it at all. That needs to be okay with you.

There are lots of things that you can do (as you'll discover in the coming chapters) to inspire, challenge and support them in this process. You might even give them a copy of this book to read.

However they feel, help them to understand that this is a learning process for you too, and you'll get it wrong sometimes. Reassure the team that when you do, you'll correct the mistake as soon as you can. And they'll have an opportunity to correct their mistakes too.

## Getting Rid of Timesheets

To make the 'work anywhere' shift, there's another significant paradigm shift I recommend...

In my humble opinion, timesheets are a complete waste of time. Get rid of them. They encourage falsification, discourage trust and measure input rather than output.

The person recording the time makes it up as they go along. We all know that before we were 'the boss' we put more time down on the 'good' jobs with a better budget than the 'crap' jobs we were working on.

Some bosses even do that now to make themselves feel better about the under-priced jobs!

To top it off, the person preparing the invoices ignores the timesheets anyway. They think, *we can't charge that,* and write a load of time off, or *we billed more than that last year,* and charge what they charged last year plus a bit more.

It goes deeper than that, though. Keeping timesheets is a fundamental breach of trust with your team and customers.

It assumes that they will slack off if you don't monitor their every move in six-minute intervals (even when they go to the toilet!). Or that your customers will get away without paying for something your team has completed for them. Or worse still, with the use of timesheets they'll pay for your hangover (when you're not working efficiently), your lack of knowledge (when you have to research something) and your incompetence (when you have to do it again).

Then there's the brigade that says, 'We only keep timesheets to measure profitability on each job,' or some other rubbish. They say they never use timesheets to price, only to monitor costs.

We know that you calculate the profit a business makes by taking away costs from sales. If you are using timesheets to measure the profit per job, ask yourself, 'What can I do if the profit is "wrong"?'

You can either increase your price or cut your costs. As you are recording time to measure profitability (and you're true to your word), timesheets have to affect the price. Otherwise, it's just a pointless measurement.

If you want to become more profitable, be better at your job. Deliver more value. Become more efficient. Don't give that away at lower prices because you have spent less time on the job!

If you have clarity over the *outputs* you want from each team member, you can focus on delivering value to your customers rather than focusing on the resources they are using.

> **If you want to become more profitable, be better at your job. Deliver more value. Become more efficient. Don't give that away at lower prices because you have spent less time on the job!**

## Do I Need to Change Contracts of Employment?

I get asked this question a lot. I'm not a lawyer, so you need to ask yours. But here's my understanding, having spoken to mine: you don't need to change your contract of employment.

Just make sure that:

- all team members have the statutory minimum leave each year without having it be interrupted by you or your team
- each team member signs to opt out of the working time directive. This then allows them to work more (excess) hours in a week if they choose to.

I'd also leave the regular working hours in the contract even though you aren't using timesheets. This is important if you ever want to go back to working 'normally', and it also helps with response times if you choose to use that as a key performance indicator (KPI).

Our contracts also include the Personal Statement of Current KPIs (PSOCK) targets in the list of duties. But, as I said, check! We'll look more at KPIs and PSOCKs in the next two chapters.

# STEP 2
# OUTLINE THE PLAN

# Step 2 – Outline the Plan

You've set the scene for your team members. There's mutual trust and respect, which allows you to give your team members a lot of freedom. They're following your lead – so now you've got to make sure you know where you're going!

If you are not clear about your goals and objectives, then you'll end up making slow progress and being distracted by popular business fads.

But once you *are* clear where you're going, you can share those ideas with the team. And they can help you get your practice to where you want it to be.

If your team do not know what direction you are heading in, they can't make decisions without you. They can't even make them with you! They need to know where you (and they) are going so they can make informed decisions about the business they are a part of.

Some accountants I work with have difficulty articulating their goals. They may know what they are, but they're scared to announce them to the world. They're frightened of other people's reactions.

A team member once told me that my goals were 'pie in the sky'. His comments just made me even more determined to make them happen! I say, let go of fear and share anyway!

# Goal Setting

There are many goal-setting techniques you can use.

**Quick Win:** There are two types of goals I'd like you to consider: business goals and personal goals. Before we break those down, start off by asking yourself some questions:

- What would I do with my practice if I knew I couldn't fail?

- What would I do if I were being courageous?

- What is a decision I am putting off in the vain hope that it will go away?

Take some time to think. Write down the answers that come to mind.

Now, let's turn those answers into goals. Here are a few examples of business goals you might consider:

- To have X team members

- To have an average fee per customer of £X

- To have costs to fees of X%

- To earn £X in annual profits

- To have team members who are well trained.

Then there are goals that are a bit more personal. They are tied to, but not directly part of, your practice's goals:

- To spend X hours with my family each week

- To own X car

- To have an income of £X

- To work X hours per week.

Your practice's goals will be the primary focus of this chapter, but do consider the impact that your business goals will have on your personal life!

Let's look at the big picture: what is your ultimate purpose for being in business? Let me give you some examples:

- To increase customer wealth
- To help your team members be the best they want to be
- To save your customers money on their taxes
- To save your customers time
- To maximise profits.

These goals don't need to be set in stone at this stage. They are your first stab at a set of goals that you can refine over time.

Remember: courage is not the absence of fear, it's the triumph over it (I pinched that from someone). Whatever you have come up with, it should scare you, excite you and motivate you to get up each morning.

> " If your team do not know what direction you are heading in, they can't make decisions without you.

## What Are KPIs?

Now that you've worked out some of those big-picture ideas, let's get to the stuff that accountants love: *measuring things*. Key Performance Indicators, or KPIs, are numbers that measure how successful your practice is in achieving its objectives. In this section, you'll find some bog-standard KPIs you should measure if you want to improve your practice.

I'll share my 'Famous Five' that I believe all practice leaders should measure. From there, we'll look at a list of 18 additional KPIs so you can pick and choose which align best with your goals.

I'm often asked how many KPIs is the 'right' number to have. If you Google this, you'll get answers from zero (don't put yourself under pressure, just go with the flow, let the universe deliver) to dozens (we are in a data-driven world, you need your finger on the pulse, you can't manage what you don't measure).

Here's my take…

*Have as many KPIs as you need to make progress!*

I measure 19 in my accountancy practice, seven in The Accountants' Mastermind and five in my personal life.

I've worked with accountants who measure just three KPIs and accountants that measure 103 – which scares the life out of me, but they love it. They have numbers for everything: they feel the need to have their finger on the pulse and know exactly what the practice is doing and about to do. They're incredibly successful (by their definition) with it, as well.

But if you want a starting point, measure the 'Famous Five' to get yourself started.

After you've measured KPIs for a few months, reflect on them. Which ones have helped you make the progress you wanted? Which ones are you ignoring or find unmotivating? Are there others you can add that are more focused? Are there too many? Not enough?

What action have you taken as a result of measuring each KPI?

If you say 'nothing', either decide you're going to take action or simply ditch it.

But be careful to check you are not just changing the numbers because you are missing the target you set yourself in the first place. It is all too easy to convince yourself the number was not right in the first place rather than do the (scary) work to achieve them.

## The Famous Five KPIs

Here's the 'Famous Five'...

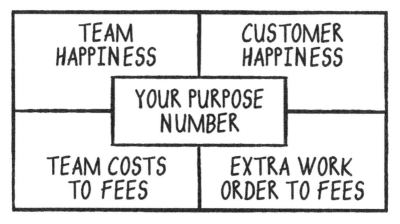

These are the five KPIs I make sure every accountancy practice I work with measures.

Here's why...

### Your 'Purpose Number'

This number helps you focus on why you're in business: that 'big picture' goal you identified above. What is the one number you can measure to monitor whether you are achieving your purpose? What's the number you can use to demonstrate to your team and your customers that you are 'getting there'?

Here are some ideas:

- Our purpose at GreenStones is to *Inspire, Challenge and Support* business owners and their teams to be the best they want to be. We measure if we are achieving that on our scorecard. We survey all our customers at least once a year and ask them to rate us on a scale of 1 to 10 for this metric. The number can't be 'audited' but, in my view, it's better than not measuring it at all. It's a constant reminder of what matters the most to our practice.

Here are some other ways to measure your purpose number:

- Measure 'increase in customer wealth' by adding up all your customers' balance sheets (business or personal) and comparing them to the previous year.

- Measure 'tax saved for your customers': how proactive you've been.

- Measure time saved for your customers by installing new systems.

Whatever your purpose is, there will be a number for it. Identify it. Measure it. Act on it!

## Team Happiness

If you have a happy team, your customers are more likely to be happy too. A happy team means happy customers.

**Quick Win:** Survey your team.

At GreenStones, we've used proprietary software in the past to measure all sorts of indicators of happiness. We've simplified this into a few simple questions that we ask through MS Forms. The main question is, 'How likely, on a scale of 1 to 10 (10 being the highest), are you to recommend working at GreenStones to your friends and family?'

We aim for an 8.5 average. Some practices aim higher and others lower. Remember: you're benchmarking against yourself – no one else.

## HOW LIKELY ARE YOU TO RECOMMEND WORKING AT GREENSTONES TO YOUR FRIENDS AND FAMILY?

★ ★ ★ ★ ★ ★ ★ ★ ⯪ ☆

The form then goes on to ask some simple feedback questions, as follows:

- What was the best thing about working at GreenStones this month?

- What was the most challenging thing about working at GreenStones this month?

- What was your biggest learning at GreenStones this month?

Here are some common objections to measuring this metric and my opinion on those arguments:

*Objection: 'The team will use it as an opportunity to moan.'*

Most people will focus on the positive, but you will of course get negative feedback. However, it's better to know what the team are moaning about so you can do something about it rather than let their issues fester. Learn from all the information you gather and use it to become a better leader.

*Objection: 'They will score me low if I upset them.'*

Yes... so don't upset them! If you have trust between you and your team, then you can have productive conflict without either party ending up 'upset'. If you believe you are being scored down because of your feedback style – change it!

*Objection: 'I should know how happy my team is without having to send a survey.'*

Certainly you should! But asking formally allows you to track this with some degree of objectivity. It shows your team you are focused on how happy they are. If this objection resonates with you then ask yourself, 'What am I trying to avoid hearing by not carrying out the survey?' Then go work on your answer.

*Objection: 'They'll lie to keep me happy and avoid confrontation.'*

If you think this, reread the section on trust. If you don't trust them, they should not be working with you.

*Objection: 'My team is always happy, so there is no need to measure it.'*

First off, I doubt that this is true! If you are never getting any constructive feedback, it may be because your team are scared to give it. It might be best to undertake an anonymous survey so you can really dig deep. But even if your team are happy, they could always be happier. There is always something you can improve. This is a pursuit, not a destination.

## Customer Happiness

How happy are your customers? This is a leading metric, a very strong indicator of the future performance of your practice.

The higher the score, the more likely your customers are to stay with you and, just as importantly, to recommend you.

**Quick Win:** Survey your customers.

GreenStones measures customer happiness at least once a year.

The main question is the Net Promoter Score (NPS) question:

'How likely are you to recommend us to your friends and family if they need accountancy services?'

The form also asks questions about our performance, perceived value for money, and the 'Purpose Number' you learned about in the 'Your Purpose Number' section above.

As above, a common objection is that customers will use the survey as an opportunity to moan. In my experience, they very rarely do.

You are better than you think you are. And if they do moan, I'd rather they moaned directly to me than to their mate down the pub. If they have a valid complaint and address it with us directly, we can put it right.

The customer survey can also be used for so much more than just getting feedback. If it is set up correctly, it is an opportunity to up-serve (cross-sell) and generate referrals. You just need to ask the right questions throughout the survey to achieve both.

## Team Costs to Fees

This is the classic metric, the one accountants seem to get most excited about. This KPI measures how productive your team is being. Obviously, the more productive they are, the more profitable you will be. But, as we'll see, this number can be manipulated, and you need to be very careful how you focus on it.

Ever since I have been an accountant there has been the 'magic' rule of thirds:

- one third overhead
- one third team costs
- one third profit

Some accountants pursue this metric with a passion.

The first thing to do is make sure you are measuring it consistently.

**Quick Win:** Decide how to calculate your costs to fees. Before we get into what the number 'should' be, let's look at the calculation. It can be simply:

$$\frac{\text{team costs}}{\text{turnover}}$$

But what makes up team cost? The whole team? Exclude administration? Include or exclude outsourcing? Contractors? Partners' wages? A market salary for the directors? Shareholder dividends?

And what makes up turnover? Total turnover? Gross Recurring Fees (GRF) only? GRF invoiced in a year? Exclude directors' billings? Include or exclude Work in Progress (WIP)?

*It really doesn't matter as long as you do it consistently.*

Pick your formula and do the same calculation month on month so you can monitor the trend. If you're not happy with the trend, take action to change it!

This is the calculation method I use at GreenStones and The Accountants' Mastermind, and the one I'll recommend to you:

$$\frac{\text{total team costs for the last 12 months}}{\text{total turnover for the last 12 months}}$$

Team costs include everything: admin, outsourcing, National Insurance (NI) contributions, pensions, etc.

We also make an adjustment for directors' commercial salaries, as most accountants pay low salaries/high dividends, and therefore the profits are not truly accurate.

We include a salary of £75,000 for each owner in the practice who does not receive a commercial salary. This salary is reduced or increased pro-rata to the days they work in the practice doing fee-generating work. For example, if a director only works four days, it is reduced to £60,000 (£75,000*0.8). Any salary costs associated with that owner already included in the profit and loss account are then added back.

Total turnover is just that: turnover for the last 12 months (adjusted for WIP) as shown per your accounts.

Using this basis, the results for the members of The Accountants' Mastermind come out somewhere between 42% and 63%. The average is 52%.

There's such a big spread as the ratio depends massively on your overall strategy: Is it 'pile 'em high, sell 'em cheap' or 'charge a premium price for a premium product'? Neither strategy is right or wrong. You just need to be conscious of which one you are pursuing.

Now you've decided how to measure your costs to fees, let's look at how the different strategies can affect this ratio. Then you can decide if you wish to pursue them.

*1. You can charge more.*

Let's start with turnover: if you increase your prices, then your turnover will go up. If you overcharge your customers and rip them off for the work you are doing, turnover will go up even more! I know lots of accountants undercharge, but you will have also seen 'gurus' who promote 'value billing' as a means to charge more than a job is actually worth. Over the years I have heard some horrendous stories around the fees charged for simple incorporations just because the tax saved was high.

But…

*You are worth more than you think you are.*

If you are on Facebook or LinkedIn, you'll have noticed the threads where accountants talk about price. Often there will be a funny meme. However, for there to be an average price, there must be the same number of accountants 'overcharging'!

One way you can make it to the magic 33% is to increase your prices (you really should!) and, as long as you are at the market rate for the services you deliver, there's nothing wrong with that.

**2. *You can do less work for the price you are charging.***

You know, 'cut corners'.

You don't fancy that much, do you? If you don't do all of the work you have quoted for, or do a substandard job, then obviously the invoices will go out quicker and your ratio will go down. This is not something I want to do, personally!

Let's move to team costs.

**3. *You can underpay your team.***

In other words, pay them less than market value and abuse their trust. Despite what you may think, team members are not on the hunt for a new job 24/7. Most trust you to pay them a fair wage for the job they are doing. If you are not careful you can take advantage of this situation and underpay your team.

Again, I don't think this is a good course of action.

**4. *You can work your team harder.***

If they worked harder (or longer) for the same pay, then they should produce more work. If they produce more work for the same cost, then your ratio will again go down. You might find short-term success with this strategy but, over the long term, you'll wear out your team and it will backfire.

5. *You can work yourself harder.*

If you do lots of fee-earning work, stay late, work weekends without paying yourself, then the KPI will come down. Your fee will go up for no corresponding increase in team costs. Again, not something I'd want to do.

I take my hat off to the firms that are charging above-average fees and/or paying less than the UK market rate for their teams in an efficient way.

For the rest of us, don't beat yourself up about the magic 33%. Work out your strategy, decide what your labour costs should be to deliver the service you want to deliver, then go for that. Compare your actual numbers against *your* budgeted number and make sure you are on track by following the trend.

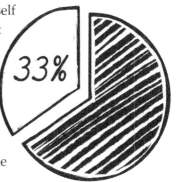

You'll save yourself a lot of stress.

## Extra Work Orders (EWOs) to Fees

Most accountants get distracted by finding new customers. It's sexy. For some it makes the adrenalin flow. However, there's an easier way to increase turnover, but takes a bit of conscious effort and belief in yourself.

You already have a bank of customers that (hopefully) know, like and trust you. Those customers already know how you work and the standard of service you provide, so they are much more likely to buy from you than someone they are meeting for the first time.

I accept it is not as sexy as chasing new customers and you might be a little bit scared they'll say no, but *focusing on up-serving is a quicker and easier way to increase fees.*

I am constantly amazed more practice owners do not focus on it.

As with team costs to fees, there is no one right way to measure EWOs, as long as you are consistent. But here's how we do it within the Mastermind community.

We work out all the extra work we have invoiced over the last 12 months. 'Extra work' is any work we didn't do in the previous 12 months, as well as new reoccurring work.

It would include the first 12 months' charges for a new payroll a customer engaged you to do; your fee for undertaking a Research and Development claim; a cashflow projection (if you don't normally do them); Independent Financial Advisor commissions; mortgage applications; etc. You then divide that number by your 'compliance fees' to get your KPI.

When we survey the members of The Accountants' Mastermind on this basis, the average result is 15%. Basically, you should be invoicing an additional 15% on top of your normal compliance fees. If you are billing less than that then you are definitely missing opportunities.

# 18 Additional KPIs

There are many other KPIs you could measure in your practice. These KPIs will ultimately be allocated to team members who will be held accountable for them.

This is not an exhaustive list. Focus on ones that are best suited for your practice.

You'll find out what to do with them later in the book to make sure you are focusing on the right actions and making progress towards your goals.

## Profit (Monthly and/or Cumulatively)

This is obvious for accountants. Add back your salary and dividend or leave it in; once again, just be consistent. Express it as an actual figure or as a percentage of turnover.

## Turnover or GRF (Monthly and/or Cumulatively)

This is the total amount invoiced in a month. You could include a Work in Progress (WIP) adjustment, if you like, or leave it out. Again, it doesn't matter provided you do it consistently. Remember: the danger of adjusting for WIP is that it might not get billed. Keep that in mind if you include it. (At GreenStones we don't include it.)

## Average Fee Per Customer

You work this out by taking total fees for the last 12 months and dividing it by the number of customers you have at the end of that 12 months.

$$\frac{\text{total fees for the last 12 months}}{\text{number of customers you have at the end of that 12 months}}$$

You can make it more complicated and use the average number of customers you have had over the last 12 months, but I don't see the point.

Note: average fees get talked about a lot in Facebook groups and on social media. The implication is always, 'the higher the average fee, the better the practice'.

But this isn't always the case as it depends on what strategy you are following ('pile 'em high, sell 'em cheap' or 'premium service'). If you're conscious of the strategy you're following and your trend, the average fee of other practices is irrelevant to you.

## Leads Generated

This is the number (quantity) or value (in fees) of new leads generated by the practice.

It's normally measured monthly, and you need to clearly define what a 'lead' is. GreenStones defines a lead as 'someone who has the initial meeting and meets our acceptable customer profile'. If they don't have a meeting with us or fit our acceptable profile, they don't count.

We measure total fees as opposed to the number of leads.

## Leads Converted

This is the number of (or value of) leads converted in the month. GreenStones counts them as converted as soon as the engagement letter is signed.

You should not be converting every lead you receive. If you are, you are either accepting substandard customers who you should not be working with or you are too cheap.

A good number to aim for is a 75% conversion rate, but I have seen practices who operate in specific niches and/or offer specialist services with a rate as low as 50%.

## Cash at Bank

This is your target cash balance. Do you want to be in credit? Have three months' reserves? Work out what you want it to be. As you know, having surplus cash on the balance sheet is just as bad (wasteful) as not having enough.

## Direct Debits Collected

This can be measured in several ways. When GreenStones was moving over from standing orders to Direct Debits (DDs), we measured the total fees collected on DD to the total fees of the practice. This encouraged the team to tackle the bigger fees first, which made the biggest impact.

You could also measure this by setting a fixed target, say, £X per month on DDs. Some practices do this, so they know their wages and overhead costs are covered each month before they open the door.

Finally, I've seen working to a set number of customers each month work successfully. Let's say you have 120 customers: you're looking to get 10 customers per month on DD and, over the course of a year, they will all be on DD.

## Debtors

There are two ways to measure this:

- the absolute amount outstanding to you at the end of the month, expressed as a value; or
- the average number of days a debtor has been outstanding.

Work it out by dividing your total debtors by your turnover and multiplying it by 365 days.

$$\frac{\text{total debtors}}{\text{turnover}} \times 365$$

You want this number to be as low as possible.

## Work in Progress (WIP)

This one is very similar to debtors – just one step back in the process. Many practices are removing it completely now by billing their customers every month in the financial year of the customer. For example, if the customer's financial year is 30 June 2022, then the accountancy fees for that year will have all been invoiced and paid before that date.

If you're not there yet, it's the amount of work you've completed that hasn't been invoiced at month end.

You can measure it the same way you measure debtors: absolutely or as days. The lower the number the better!

$$\frac{\text{total WIP}}{\text{turnover}} \times 365$$

## Productivity/Write-Offs

If you keep timesheets, you can measure your productivity ratio and/or the amount you write off each month.

As I discussed previously, there are so many ways this KPI can be abused and manipulated that it hardly seems worth mentioning. It's here for completeness in case it appeals to you. (I hope it doesn't!)

$$\frac{\text{productive hours}}{\text{available productive hours}}$$

## Customers Lost

Some accountants wear it as a badge of honour that they never lose a customer. I smile when I see that and question if those practices are putting their prices up often enough and if they're innovating enough. Your practice should keep changing, developing and improving. Some customers won't like that as they prefer the 'old' way. The ones that don't like it will leave.

That being said, we still want to make sure we're delivering exceptional service, and we're explaining the changes to our customers so they understand what the benefits are for them. And if we don't do that and they leave, we have some learnings to discover.

GreenStones measures the total value of customers lost in the month. We separate them between customers lost through no fault of our own (retirement, liquidation, etc) and those we lose to a 'professional clearance' letter. Then each month we review them and see what mistakes (if any) we made in the relationship.

## Learning Points

'Learning point' is the polite name we have for 'mistakes made'.

This one is a little more challenging to measure, and you need to make sure you have clarity on what is and what isn't a learning point.

GreenStones' definition of a **learning point** is 'anything we find when we review the accounts that would stop the accounts going to the customer'.

It could be as significant as the bank not being appropriately reconciled, all the way down to a full stop missing from the end of a sentence. (We'd never send a set of accounts to a customer

61

if there was a spelling or grammatical error!)

If in the review we spot anything that means the accounts can't go to a customer, then that counts as a learning point.

As the number of sets of accounts produced varies each month, we can't measure the total number of learning points in a month. We must measure the average number of learning points per job to get a consistent measure. The calculation is total learning points divided by the total number of accounts produced.

It doesn't matter what the definition is for you if it's clear and your team is held accountable for it.

You should keep a list of all the learning points you discover at review. You can then come together as a team once a month to share the learning points to make sure everyone in the team learns from the mistakes that have been made.

Most of the GreenStones team now operate at less than one learning point per job. With new team members the target is set at six to start with and then reduced as they get used to our systems.

## Turnaround Times

This KPI measures how quickly you produce annual accounts and/or VAT returns. It is usually measured in days. Practices often use it as a measure of efficiency, as the quicker you can turn a set of accounts around, the more profitable they are likely to be and the less WIP you will be carry on your balance sheet.

GreenStones measures the number of days it takes to produce a set of accounts from the day the records arrive (books in) to the day the final accounts go to the customer to be signed.

We remove any days where we're waiting for the customer to respond to us. There are three times this happens:

- when we're waiting for missing information after a job has been booked in
- when the meeting is booked to review the accounts
- when we're waiting for further information from the customer after the draft accounts have been reviewed at a meeting.

The time taken to complete any of those three is outside of our control. I can accept that we can reduce the time by communicating with the customer better but, ultimately, how long they take to provide information or when they want to have the meeting is up to them.

A word of caution: be careful of being sucked into the 'accounts filed within X days of year end' KPI some 'gurus' and accountants promote. This is completely outside of your control, not only for the three reasons mentioned above, but also for the delivery of the records to you. If the customer cares about it, they will do it. If not, you'll be banging your head against a brick wall for no reason!

## Development Activities

Assume that your team wants to develop. They want to keep their knowledge up to date. If they don't, they probably shouldn't be working for you.

Over the course of a few months, it becomes very difficult to remember what training you've done on the job as each day blurs into the next. Record every training so that it can be reviewed and shared with the whole team.

At GreenStones, we describe a **development activity** as something that takes about an hour and helps you do a better job.

It specifically excludes continuing professional development (CPD) and exams, because the team should be doing them anyway as a basic requirement of their job. I want the team to get a wider experience that they can share with our customers. These activities are most often Xero/Excel training, ideas, business books read and webinars attended.

Every team member has a target of at least one development activity per month. Some of the team members who are developing to be customer-facing have two or three a month.

One of the most unusual development activities we've ever had was watching the film, *We Bought a Zoo*. The film stars Matt Damon and – you guessed it – he buys a zoo. Needless to say, the venture does not go according to plan. In overcoming various obstacles, the character tells his son, 'You know, sometimes all you need is 20 seconds of insane courage. Just literally 20 seconds of embarrassing bravery, and I promise you something great will come of it.'

A team member who had watched the film used that concept of '20 seconds of embarrassing bravery' to motivate them to talk to someone at a networking event. At the end of the conversation, they got an agreement to a meeting and subsequently that prospect became a customer. All because they watched a film. I think that counts as a development activity!

## Ideas Generated

There's very little benefit in learning new things if they don't generate ideas to improve your practice and the businesses of the customers you work with.

At GreenStones, we have a suggestion box scheme. We measure the number of ideas generated each month from the learning activities and record that as a KPI. That way we know the development activities are generating ideas.

## Ideas Implemented

There's no point in undertaking development activities and generating ideas if you're not going to implement them. This KPI monitors how many ideas that have been generated get implemented.

It's important to share this with the team to demonstrate their ideas are being listened to and being implemented. Explain to the team why certain ideas are or are not being implemented. The best time to do this is when the decision is made (vocally in a meeting or via one of the messaging apps if you are working remotely). The explanation helps your team to understand why certain things happen or don't happen. It also helps them improve the ideas generated as they can learn from the feedback you give them.

Be careful not to become the bottleneck in ideas being implemented.

## Proactive Calls

'Proactive' is one of those buzzwords that gets bandied about, but how do you know if you actually are proactive? This KPI can help you *demonstrate* that you're proactive to your customers and your potential customers.

You can decide what proactive means to you and measure that instead. We describe a **proactive call** as any call that the customer is not expecting. They are designed to add value to the customer over and above what we promise in the engagement letter.

Our best customers get at least one proactive call a month. Others get one a quarter. You need to decide your own service levels.

I've suggested for a long time that a truly proactive accountant would never receive a telephone call or email about a problem from a customer. They would've already solved the problem before the customer knew it existed!

Of course, that's not entirely possible. Things will always happen unexpectedly (death, divorce, illness, etc) that mean the customer will have to make contact. But it's still a nice ambition to have.

## Outstanding Items/Jobs/Tasks on Control Panel

Every team member should have clarity on what they are supposed to do and when.

We use a control panel on our practice management software to monitor the job stages, but you could easily substitute in to-do lists or Excel spreadsheets if that's what you prefer. Use whatever you want to plan and monitor the work in your practice. The closer you can get to zero, the better!

# What Period Do You Set Targets For?

Now that you've decided which KPIs you want to implement,

you need to set a timeframe for accomplishing them.

I have loose goals around a ten-year timeframe (walk Land's End to John O'Groats, be debt-free, for example) but so much can happen in ten years. Is it really worth planning for them now? For me, it's not. But if it appeals to you, then please do.

I think three years is a much more interesting time frame. Three years is only 12 quarters or 36 months. That, to me, seems more immediate. I have some broad-brush numbers for three years and then go all-in and really focus on the next 12 months.

My advice is to set goals and aspirations (as well as the numbers you need to achieve them) for the next 12 months.

I then break those 12-month numbers into monthly targets and the important ones into weekly amounts. I only get into the detail of weekly reporting if I believe I can affect the values on a weekly basis.

You could then break the numbers down even further into daily or even hourly targets (telephone calls, for example) but, for me, that's a step too far.

Review the numbers you're measuring every six months or so. Are they still relevant? Are they still helping you achieve your goals? Are you still taking action because of them? If not, you need to revaluate either your actions or your goals, or both, to bring them into alignment.

## Record Your Numbers

Once you've determined what you want to measure and how you want to measure it, you need to keep records of how you're measuring up. I call this the Business Statement of Current KPIs, or BSOCK.

There are many software packages out there that will enable you to record and monitor your KPIs. Don't let yourself get distracted by all the options. Don't put off measuring your KPIs until you find the perfect software – you won't! They all have their flaws.

To date, having played with lots of software, I've found nothing better than Excel. It requires manual data entry, but it works. The team know how to use it and we can trust the numbers.

 Download a BSOCK spreadsheet template at
WWW.BANISHTHEBOTTLENECK.COM/FREEGIFTSFROMSIMON

As you will see in the example on the next page, you have the months across the top and the KPIs down the left-hand side. You will also notice under each KPI you have a person's name(s) so you can see who is accountable for that KPI.

Each month has a column for the actual number, target number, and the difference. This allows you to see at a glance the targets that have been hit and the ones that have been missed.

In the example, you will see a 'summary' grouping called 'Last Quarter'. This helps you avoid snap decisions based on the individual months, as those results can fluctuate quite dramatically. GreenStones reports trends for each quarter, 6-month period, and 12-month period.

The last thing to point out to you is the ability to add comments to each of the cells. You can add notes about what targets were hit or missed, actions you are going to take for next month, or the breakdown and description of the number in the cell.

We're in the process of linking the spreadsheet to various sources of data via PowerBI. It's too soon to share how successful this has been, but fingers crossed it will be more effective than manually finding and typing in the numbers.

| | A B | C | D | E | F | G | H | I | J |
|---|---|---|---|---|---|---|---|---|---|
| 1 | BSOCKS | | | | | | | | |
| 2 | | | | | | | | | |
| 3 | | | | Last Quarter | | | | Month 12 | |
| 4 | | | Actual | Target | Difference | | Actual | Target | Difference |
| 5 | | | | | | | | | |
| 6 | Purpose Number | | | | | | | | |
| 7 | Director 1 | | 455,000 | 450,000 | 5,000 | | 145,000 | 150,000 | (5,000) |
| 8 | | | | | | | | | |
| 9 | Team Happiness | | | | | | | | |
| 10 | Director 1 | | 27.0 | 25.5 | 1.5 | | 9.2 | 8.5 | 0.7 |
| 11 | | | | | | | | | |
| 12 | Customer happiness | | 27.4 | 27.0 | 0.4 | | 9.2 | 9.0 | 0.2 |
| 13 | Director 1 | | | | | | | | |
| 14 | | | | | | | | | |
| 15 | Team Costs/Fees | | | | | | | | |
| 16 | Director 1 | | 154% | 126% | (28)% | | 50% | 42% | (8)% |
| 17 | | | | | | | | | |
| 18 | EWOs/Fee | | | | | | | | |
| 19 | Director 1 | | 28% | 45% | (17)% | | 8% | 15% | (7)% |
| 20 | | | | | | | | | |
| 21 | Fees Invoiced | | 85,500 | 87,000 | (1,500) | | 28,000 | 29,000 | (1,000) |
| 22 | Director 1 | | 15,500 | 15,000 | 500 | | 6,500 | 5,000 | 1,500 |
| 23 | Team Member 1 | | 31,000 | 30,000 | 1,000 | | 8,000 | 10,000 | (2,000) |
| 24 | Team Member 2 | | 16,000 | 18,000 | (2,000) | | 4,500 | 6,000 | (1,500) |
| 25 | Team Member 3 | | 23,000 | 24,000 | (1,000) | | 9,000 | 8,000 | 1,000 |
| 26 | | | | | | | | | |
| 27 | Profit | | 20,750 | 22,500 | (1,750) | | 6,750 | 7,500 | (750) |
| 28 | | | | | | | | | |
| 29 | Learning Points | | 12.0 | 10.5 | (1.5) | | 4.0 | 3.5 | (0.5) |
| 30 | Team Member 1 | | 3.0 | 3.0 | 0.0 | | 1.0 | 1.0 | 0.0 |
| 31 | Team Member 2 | | 2.0 | 1.5 | (0.5) | | 0.5 | 0.5 | 0.0 |
| 32 | Team Member 3 | | 7.0 | 6.0 | (1.0) | | 2.5 | 2.0 | (0.5) |
| 33 | | | | | | | | | |
| 34 | Leads Generated | | 5 | 6 | (1) | | 2 | 2 | 0 |
| 35 | Director 1 | | 3 | 3 | 0 | | 1 | 1 | 0 |
| 36 | Team Member 2 | | 2 | 3 | (1) | | 1 | 1 | 0 |
| 37 | | | | | | | | | |

*Example of a BSOCK*

The major point here is that you need some sort of system to track KPIs, whether as a BSOCK like ours or in some other form.

# Determine Your Values

With those details settled, let's once again zoom out to the big picture of what you want your business to be. If we just monitored numbers, it would be like keeping score in a game but not having any rules. The players could make the rules up as they went along.

You are giving your team members a vast amount of freedom in how they do their work, but it's essential that they still operate within your values, otherwise they might cut corners or even break the law to hit their numbers!

But if you have well-defined values that you all share, the team can make decisions to support each other and your clients. They'll have some guidance they can fall back on. Ultimately, they'll be making the same (or very similar) decisions as you would if you were there, as the team are working to your agenda.

I recommend a four-step process for determining your values: Discover, Define, Develop and Deploy. You can do most of these steps on your own if you'd like, but they can also make a good activity for the Away Day we'll talk about in the next chapter.

## Discover

**Quick Win**: Brainstorm words that describe you and your practice. Write down as many as you can to start with. Keep going until you have at least 15–20, but 30 is better and 50 is ideal!

For the grammar nerds amongst us, try to list words from a variety of parts of speech. (If doing so isn't useful to you, do feel free to scrap this portion!)

- Verbs – these are action words that tell what your people

do, such as plan, adapt, or imagine.

- Abstract nouns – characteristics that you can't touch, such as integrity, consistency or bravery.

- Adjectives – descriptive words, such as thoughtful, proactive or goal-oriented.

It sometimes helps to think of situations where you have been at your best – stories you and the team like to share about the successes the practice has had.

Once you have a good list, pick your seven or so favourite words.

You might like to take a little break here and ask the team which ones they like and that they think are critical to the way you work. You can also ask them to come up with stories to demonstrate how the team have lived by that value or rule in the last six months or so.

Once you have completed this review, you'll probably find two or three that no longer resonate. Drop those so you end up with no more than five. (More than that and your team will struggle to remember them.)

## Define

Next, you need to get clarity on what the words mean. The same word means different things to different people.

Write a definition for each value and again share them with the team. Allow them to help you refine the definition. For example, some might see *honesty* and *integrity* as synonymous. Others might think that integrity also means proactively living according to values rather than simply 'not telling lies'. By the end of this process, you'll have a clear and precise definition of each word.

*A values board at GreenStones*

## Develop

Once you have decided your values and defined them, share with the team how you expect them to live by the values. What does it look like?

Share examples of situations, internal or customer-facing, that they are commonly involved in. Discuss what action you'd like them to take in line with the values.

## Deploy

Here's what you'll often see in a corporate office: the values are printed out on a piece of paper. They're laminated and stuck on the wall for everyone to see. If there's a reception desk, they're stuck up behind there too. Now, everyone can see them when they come in.

No! No! No! A complete waste of time.

You need to live them and breathe them each and every day. Here are some ideas you can use to make sure the team are on board.

### *The GreenStones Mug*

One of my favourite ideas for keeping values in front of the team members is to have them printed on mugs that I customise and give to each person.

Ask your graphics designer to create an attractive image using your values. Add each team member's name to the design so they're more personal.

Go to one of the websites where you can create a personalised item (such as https://www.vistaprint.co.uk), choose a wraparound design and upload each jpeg file.

Each mug will cost about £15, and every time a team member has a drink, they'll be reminded of the company values.

This is far better than sticking values on the wall where no one takes a blind bit of notice of them!

Other ideas:

- Play games around values.

- Add them to your website.

- Share them as part of the recruitment process.

- Spend time talking about them at the induction.

- Pick a value for each team meeting and discuss what it means.

There are lots of other ways you can come up with to ingrain them into your working environment. Be creative!

# STEP 3
## CONFIRM AND
## CONVERSE WITH THE TEAM

# Step 3 – Confirm and Converse With the Team

Let's reflect and celebrate how far you've come. Many accountants and business owners don't get this far. They're not brave enough to share their ambitions and goals. They're not brave enough to be accountable.

You now have some fantastic goals for yourself and for your practice. At this point, the temptation is to try to implement all of these goals on your own. To micromanage. *To make yourself the bottleneck.*

Don't do it. This is the point at which you most need your team members' support.

My favourite way to get team members on board is at a team Away Day.

## Just Get Started

There's nothing remarkable about GreenStones' story and the way we started developing as a team.

We simply spent a day together and shared the goals as a team. There was no tree-hugging, raft-building or creating paper towers. Just real conversations that made an impact on the practice and on the lives of the people involved in it.

I'm going to give you a loose agenda you can follow if you choose to do it this way. Spend a day away from the office and get to know each other in a different environment.

I know you might find the prospect of this a little daunting. It's so tempting to dash off an email, produce a memo or issue a notice. That may be efficient, but it's definitely not as effective as being together for the day.

There's a whole list of things that you can fear...

- What if they don't like my ideas?
- What if they think I'm nuts?
- What if they argue with each other?
- What if X says something stupid?
- What if *I* say something stupid?
- What if X gets mad?
- What if the food at the hotel is rubbish?
- What if a customer desperately needs us?

...but these fears are usually unfounded.

I've run hundreds of Away Days over the years for our team, customers of GreenStones, and the accountancy practices I work with. I can't think of one occasion where any of the above has adversely affected the outcome of the day together.

The irony is, even when they go wrong, they are going right! Here's why: often the elephant in the room is being addressed. Whatever is going 'wrong' is an opportunity to learn and develop as a team. You have a chance to seize that moment and make a change. That moment then becomes part of your story.

On one Away Day I facilitated it was clear that one of the team members (let's call her Dianne) had a problem. It was clear that she was not enjoying the day and not contributing.

At lunchtime I made sure I got a chance to speak to Dianne one-on-one and she assured me everything was okay. It clearly wasn't, and one or two other team members were beginning to notice it too.

Many people in the room had got the impression Dianne did not care about them or the work she was doing. That was far from the truth.

I decided to change the first exercise after lunch to draw out the challenges the team were experiencing. It didn't take long! Dianne burst into a fit of rage and very aggressively informed us that we were focusing on the wrong things. We were waffling about talking about our feelings, but our customers hadn't been getting the quality of work that they deserved.

Then Dianne did something even more brave. She shared with us that trauma from her past made it especially difficult for her to speak up in this manner.

When she had finished, I simply asked, 'What do you want instead?'

After a pause that felt like a lifetime, she told me (and the room) what she wanted. There was stunned silence before the room burst into conversation.

Dianne's outburst had broken the ice and given the team permission to share. If she could speak up about what she felt needed to change, they could, as well! The practice owners got to hear what the whole team *really* thought that afternoon.

In the end, they agreed to create a new standard checklist to make sure the accounts system worked properly and to a higher standard… all because Dianne was brave enough to get mad.

## Before the Away Day

Occasionally, situations like Dianne's arise that are completely unexpected. Those can be the best kinds of Away Days. However, usually you'll need to do a bit of planning in order to get the results you want from the day.

It's often useful to get your team's perspective on a situation before you pull together your agenda. It's important to direct their thinking so that you get the most value from the day. This helps your team feel involved and be a part of the process. A simple way to do this is to issue a feedback form asking questions directed at what they want to achieve.

Download an example of an Away Day feedback form for you to build on at
WWW.BANISHTHEBOTTLENECK.COM/FREEGIFTSFROMSIMON

So, if you're going to be talking about the objectives of the practice over the next 12 months, you might ask questions like:

- How do you think we've performed as a practice in the last 12 months?

- As a practice, what have we achieved in the last 12 months?

- How clear are you on the goals of the practice for the next 12 months?

- What ideas do you have on how the practice can be improved in the next two months?

- What would you like to achieve on our Away Day?

Don't expect revolutionary answers. Some will write *War and*

*Peace*. Other team members will need to be chased to fill it in with three-word answers. Both are okay. This is just to get the juices flowing.

## Objectives

What's the objective of the day? Define one to three things you want to achieve by being together. These could include:

- Set the goals for next year.
- Integrate the values into the practice.
- Build on trust between the team members.
- Celebrate the success of the last year.
- Share the new KPIs you are going to be measuring.

Share these objectives with the team, along with all the details for the day, like:

- Start and finish times.
- Location.
- What you'll be doing for food (often the most important).
- Travel arrangements, if there are any.

In any communication, remember that the team members may be nervous about what's going to happen, especially if it's the first time you've run an event like this. If having Away Days is new to you too, mention this to your team to put them at ease.

# The Agenda

You can, of course, create any agenda you want. What follows is my suggested agenda that I've used successfully.

One thing that's not negotiable, though, is an action planning sheet. Have a flip chart at the front of the room and every time a possible action comes up, it goes on the sheet. You can then use this to summarise the day and create your actual actions at the end of the day. An A4 sheet can work in a pinch, but your team won't be able to see it. If it is big and at the front of the room it acts as a constant reminder of why you are in the room: to take action to make things better.

## Ice-Breaker

In any meeting, the sooner someone speaks, the more likely they are to contribute to the meeting. You just have to get them going.

Go round the room and ask everyone to share one word that describes how they think or feel about the day. If you have time, three words are even better.

Some team members will be shy with their answer, some will be clever and some team members will copy the people that went before them. All of those answers are okay. The most important thing is that they have simply spoken up.

But do listen. Sometimes they reveal more than they think.

It's okay to ask someone to expand on their answer, but don't dwell too long on any one person. Write the words on a flip chart if you like. If there's a theme to the answers (nerves is a common one), acknowledge that at the end by saying how interesting it is that lots of people feel the same way. If you think that this nervousness might pose a challenge during the day, find out what you can do during the day to help... then do it!

Remember *you* need to share as well because *you're* part of the team and the meeting! But never go first. Instead, let *them* lead the conversation.

---

**Quick Win**

If you are struggling to get team members to contribute to your meetings, it might be because you have not given them permission to speak. The sooner you do that, via an ice-breaker, the more likely they are to contribute.

The one-word/three-word check-in is not always necessary at every meeting. Sometimes you might want to start off a little bit more light-heartedly.

Here are a few of my favourite questions you can use at the start of a meeting to get people going and improve trust.

- What is the strangest thing you have in the boot of your car?
- What is your favourite sitcom?
- If you were on death row, what would your last meal be?
- Where would you go if you could fly anywhere?
- What superpower would you most like?

I'm sure you can come up with some of your own as well.

Get team members to share a few of their answers so everyone can laugh together.

---

## Trust Exercise

Depending on what you're focusing on during the day, you can build ice-breakers into trust exercises.

For example, you can get everyone to share their favourite hobbies, holiday destination or food. All of these are gentle openers which will get people talking. The team will find out things they never knew about each other and there's always a laugh along the way.

Here's how it works...

Start with talking about something low-risk like hobbies,

holidays and destinations. Then move up to something more challenging, like their favourite thing to do at work, if they have any brothers or sisters, proudest childhood moment, proudest adult moment, and then finish off with their weakest and strongest qualities.

> **The sooner someone speaks, the more likely they are to contribute to the meeting.**

Take your team through this process over the course of a day and you'll have learned and shared a great deal about one another and built a great deal of trust. It might feel a little scary at first, but it's always worth it.

## Celebrate Successes

How often do you celebrate what you've achieved as a team? In most practices, it's not very often (if at all)!

This is your chance to help the team recognise how much they've achieved over the last 12 months and how different your practice is compared to the start of the year. It also helps energise the meeting.

Depending on how big your team is you can split them into groups and ask them to come up with as many changes and improvements in the practice as they can in, say, ten minutes.

You'll be amazed at what team members come up with and remember. Once you have your list, you might want to have a conversation about the things that have worked really well in the practice in the last 12 months to round it off.

By this time the team will be engaged with the day – some more than others, of course, but they should all be contributing.

You've set the scene, and my advice would be to take a quick break. Stretch your legs and let the learnings from the first section sink in.

## Share the Vision

Let's start coming up with some actions as a team to move the practice forward.

It's very important that you share your vision with the team to make sure they know where you're going. The rest of the day will be focused on achieving that.

You should share the KPIs you created earlier along with any other goals or objectives you have. Allow the team to ask questions and to challenge your thinking. Remember that they're asking questions to learn. This is a good sign. It means they trust you.

As you learnt in the previous chapter, your team need to ask the questions (Patrick Lencioni called it conflict) to get commitment to the decision being made. Welcome the questions and embrace them even though it may feel a little scary.

You'll also want to introduce the concept of team member KPIs (which we will talk about shortly) so they can start to see how it all fits together. You don't need to share them or set them at this point. Just mention that someone needs to be accountable (nearly always you to start with!) for each of the practice's KPIs.

## Share the Current Situation

So now they know where they're going, you need to establish where you are.

|  | POSITIVE | NEGATIVE |
|---|---|---|
| **INTERNAL** | <u>S</u>TRENGTHS | <u>W</u>EAKNESSES |
| **EXTERNAL** | <u>O</u>PPORTUNITIES | <u>T</u>HREATS |

*A SWOT analysis*

The best way to do this is to undertake a **SWOT analysis**: ask the team to share what they think are the practice's strengths, weaknesses, opportunities, and threats. After they've shared their thoughts, establish if there are any actions that the analysis can drive. Record it on the big paper so you can review it at the end of the day.

You should also share any information they don't currently have which they might find useful. Profit and loss account, balance sheet position, and cashflow forecasts, for example. The more information they have, the better informed their decisions will be.

## Share the Values

Make sure the team understands the boundaries and culture of your practice. What you'll share depends on what work you've completed on this in the past.

If you've already spent time Discovering, Defining, Developing and Deploying your values as a group, your team may only need a refresher at this point.

You might choose to revisit the stories you have chosen to see if there are some more up-to-date ones you can now use, or look at how you're deploying them in your practice to keep them at the front of people's minds.

If you've never shared your values before, now is the time!

You can hand the momentum over to your team. You can ask the team to define them. You might be amazed at what they think your choice of words means compared to your thinking! The conversation can very often be a place to have some lighted-hearted fun.

Here's how you do it…

Share one of your values and then ask each team member to write down what they think it means on a piece of paper. Give them 30 seconds or so to do it. Then ask a few team members to share. Once you have listened to the answers you can then reshare what you want and think it means so the team will better understand your thinking.

Next, develop the values further by asking the team to share their stories of how the practice lives by the values. Again, I'm often surprised by the stories I've never heard before. This is also a really good trust exercise.

If you feel strong in both of those areas, you can ask the team about who could better deploy the values. What ideas do they have to keep them 'front of mind' each day when they're at work?

I shared some earlier in the book and I'll be discussing 'games' later so you'll be armed with some ideas in case they draw a blank.

*Me and my team at an Away Day*

## Anything Else?

Hopefully, anything you think needs to be discussed has already been brought up as part of the conversations up to this point. But if not, here is the time to toss it in.

It might be something from the feedback form, or some software you want to share, or a conversation you want to have about the performance of the practice.

## Set the Actions

This is the most important part of the day. It's where the action happens and where you make real progress.

But be careful: *never commit to anything at this point that you're not 100% confident you're going to do*. It is fatal if you say you're going to do something and then change your mind.

It's far better to have 'possible' actions and then confirm them later than have actions that never get implemented. Otherwise, next time, they won't believe you, and the trust will be broken.

A good way of running this part of the agenda is to grab the action-planning sheet you've been using all day and then ask each team member what their favourite action is.

If you're short of time, or have a lot of people, you can break them into groups and ask them to come up with a group one.

If they struggle to come up with one, change the question to:

*Which new action do you think will make the most impact on the practice?*

Or flip it around and ask your team members to remove the worst ones or the ones they don't want to support.

> **Never commit to anything that you're not 100% confident you're going to do.**

Narrow the list down to a number between one and five. You need to make sure you can implement them in a reasonable time scale (say, 3–6 months). Any that will be implemented at some point (just not yet) can be kept and revisited in the future.

Make sure that you clearly define each action, set a deadline for it, and decide who is responsible for seeing it through. If you can, let the person who thought of the idea implement it! That way it stays off your to-do list and gives them ownership of the original problem. If that is not possible, make sure you delegate as much of the implementation as possible to your team.

## Wrap Up

The temptation now is to bolt for the pub! But put that on hold for one minute.

Everyone in the room must get 'closure' from the day. Just like you started the day with everyone sharing something, you need to finish the day the same way.

*Here is Roger Stone (the 'Stone' in GreenStones) along with some of the team at the first ever GreenStones Away Day in 2003. If you look closely, you will see some wine glasses. The wine was served at the end!*

Ask each team member how they feel about the day. You might ask them to share one word or their top insight or action. It's up to you, but they *all* need to speak.

Then you can wrap up and bolt to the pub. As a team. Buzzing with energy. Ready to go.

You should notice a buzz in the office in the days after the Away Day...

# Frequently Asked Questions

*Do I need slides?*

If you feel more supported with slides, then use them, but you don't need them. Just follow the agenda laid out in this section. It works! Use the flip chart if you need to write anything down so people can see and remember it.

*Is there a maximum number of team members you can have on an Away Day?*

The simple answer is no. I have run Away Days for as few as four team members all the way up to 63 team members. A larger group just means you need to split the bigger group into smaller groups for many of the exercises and appoint a spokesperson. With larger groups you might need a loudhailer to be heard over the noise!

*How long should the meeting be?*

It's best if the meeting lasts for a whole day. Having lunch together and chatting during the breaks helps to build camaraderie. If you don't believe you can spare a full day, then do as much as you can, but never less than half a day (that just isn't worth it). Start right after the morning school run if you can.

*Who should be there?*

Everybody, including the office cat or dog.

*Should it be held on-site or off-site?*

Off-site. Always. Having the meeting off-site in a hotel is head and shoulders better than being in your office, even if you have the most luxurious Google-inspired offices in the world. Your team will think more clearly, creatively and openly off-site. And most importantly, *you* will be different off-site too!

*Do I need an outside facilitator?*

If you have the budget, a skilled facilitator can enable you to be a part of the team and work with them on the exercises. The facilitator won't have your team bias and should be able to draw the best out of each conversation.

If you don't have the budget, then by all means do it yourself. You'll deliver what you want, and you'll invest less time as you will not have to brief and debrief a facilitator.

Remember, whatever you decide to do, the most important thing is to follow through with the action steps that you have created together!

# STEP 4:
## KNOW WHAT TO GET OFF YOUR PLATE

# Step 4 – Know What to Get Off Your Plate

You have built trust with your team. You have relaxed your hold on when and where your team works. You have worked together to define your practice's vision.

Now step out of your team members' way and let them be the best they want to be!

In this chapter, you will learn the art of delegating. There are three main ways I want you to learn to do this. The first one, TARR, is a quick win that you can begin to implement **today**. The others will require some time up front. But believe me, it will be worth it when you are no longer micromanaging every aspect of your practice!

## Removing Yourself as the Bottleneck

Start thinking about how you're going to remove yourself as the bottleneck in the practice. Start delegating the work you don't enjoy doing, or don't do effectively, to the team members who can do the best job of it.

The reason most accountants are poor at delegating is that we like to be heroes. We've been taught from a very early age that you get rewarded for knowing the right answer. This causes a problem when a team member comes to you with a question. If you jump in and answer it straight away (I know it's often quicker in the short-term), it teaches the team member to come to you and ask you again next time. It gets work off their desk faster and you then reward that as they are more productive.

However, the downside is that you become less and less productive yourself and start working more and more hours. Not clever! To solve the problem, you need to get out of ego.

You need to delegate.

Here are my recommendations for learning to do that.

## Quick Win: TARR

The TARR Matrix is a brilliant tool to avoid taking on team members' problems. It is quick and easy to implement. As you do so, you will see your team members grow in both *confidence* and *competence*.

I used it so much at GreenStones that I had a copy on the wall behind my desk. If a team member came to me with a question or problem I would always ask, 'What do you recommend?' or 'What's your advice?' or 'What do you want instead?'

> *Ultimately, all they needed was reassurance they were not about to make a mistake.*

Over time, they would learn to only come and ask me *if they had already come up with a solution.* Ultimately, all they needed was reassurance they were not about to make a mistake.

Here's how it works. The

matrix helps you visualise four degrees of delegation: Tell, Ask, Recommend and Report.

For each task you delegate, the team member needs to know exactly where they are on the matrix. You should communicate this to them during the delegation process.

On the left-hand side of the matrix, you have the team member's confidence rated low to high. This is your assessment of the team member's confidence in their ability to do the assigned task.

Along the bottom, you have the team member's competence to carry out the task, again, rated low to high.

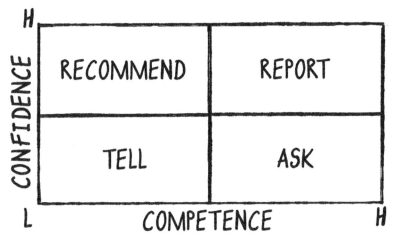

*Degrees of delegation*

As you will see, depending on how you rate them, you will choose to take different actions.

## Tell: Low Competence, Low Confidence

You know the feeling: you walk up to the photocopier and it's not working. You ask if anyone has reported it to the service company. No one has. Your heart sinks. You ask why not, and no one seems to know whose job this is or how to even go about getting it fixed. The easiest thing seems to be to report it yourself. Don't do it! Delegate instead.

Team members in this box need to be explicitly told what to do. They don't yet have the confidence to take the initiative or have the competence to complete a task independently. You have to spot the problem and then tell them what action to take. Obviously, from a delegation point of view, this is not an ideal place to be. You need to work on giving them the competence or confidence to do the task.

You can help with competence by training them to do the task. It could be as simple as writing out the system for them to follow.

Once you have trained them you may need to support them with the task the first few times. But, eventually, this process will build their confidence.

## Ask: Low Confidence, High Competence

Next up we have team members who are competent but with low confidence. You know, the team members that check with you... about everything.

They'll spot the photocopier has gone wrong and will come and ask you what to do about it. They know what to do, but they just won't have the confidence to implement it without you telling them. Of course, you deliver the answer (as you always do) and you teach them to ask you again next time!

And the next time. And the next time. And the next time.

Here's what you need to do instead. You need to support them and help them believe in themselves. Inspire them to be better than they currently are. You need to help them work within their 'can-do zone'.

**The Three Zones of Learning**

The first step is to become aware of the three zones of learning. Everybody has these zones and, no doubt, you'll recognise them in yourself too...

Comfort Zone – This is the zone you reside in most of the time. It's the zone you'll find yourself in most often when you're not being challenged or inspired to be anything more. You carry out your daily habits within it.

Crisis Zone – Furthest from your Comfort Zone is your Crisis Zone. This is when you're asked to do something which fills you with dread and, often, the result is that you take no effective action. Imagine if you went to your team and asked them to raise a million pounds of investment for your company. They would never have imagined such a challenge and would go into their Crisis Zone, resulting in no ability to act upon the delegated task. If you delegate a task to your team and see no action being taken, you need to ask yourself whether the task has taken them from their Comfort Zone straight into their Crisis Zone.

Can-Do Zone – This is the zone you need to get your team members into, where you can challenge and inspire them to achieve results. You need to allow them to spend some of their time in their Comfort Zone, but never be afraid to push them into their Can-Do Zone. The trick is to avoid pushing them beyond this zone and into the Crisis Zone.

If a team member feels they are in their Can-Do Zone, over time, they will develop their confidence and move up into the report area… and the task is off your desk!

## Recommend: High Confidence, Low Competence

This my favourite type of team member, although working with them can be a little scary at times. They have confidence in their abilities and are looking to grow. They might be ambitious. But they don't always know their limitations!

They spot the photocopier isn't working, they come and tell you and they make a recommendation on what to do next.

They might not always get it right, though, because they are working on their competence.

How do you move team members into this box? You do this by becoming conscious of the questions they ask and, instead of delivering the answer on a platter, ask this question...

**'What do you recommend?'**

*You've suddenly flipped the responsibility and provided them with the trust and challenge to answer the question for themselves.*

As a result, the more times you ask this, the more likely it is that your team members will no longer come to you with a question. Instead, they'll come to you with their own recommendation and solution to the problem.

## Report: High Confidence, High Competence

You want as many team members in this box as possible: confident and competent.

You only find out that the photocopier is broken when the team member tells you they've spoken to the support company and the photocopier will be fixed tomorrow. Better still, you don't even get told the photocopier has been broken until they report at the monthly meeting that the photocopier has gone wrong X times and they **recommend** you get a new one to save on the continued maintenance cost.

The more times you ask the 'recommend' question, the quicker your team members will end up in this box. The second-best question you can ask your team members will once again flip the level of delegated responsibility. If a team member has a problem with something, you should ask them:

**'What do you want instead?'**

By doing this you instantly turn a negative into a positive and challenge them to come up with a solution to the problem. Often, they will be able to provide you with the answer.

## Long Game: 'Stop-Doing' Lists

A more strategic way of removing yourself as the bottleneck involves a little more time and effort. It involves analysing what you're doing and then consciously deciding if you're the most effective person to do that job.

Here's how it works...

As well as the inevitable to-do list you have, you also need a 'Stop-Doing' list. That list contains all the things you do in your practice.

That's right – **all** the things you do. Not just the ones you want to stop doing.

You can compile the list by keeping a diary or simply sitting down and brainstorming a list. You could even ask your team to come up with a list for you, as well. It's up to you.

Then, for each item on the list, you ask yourself...

'Does this actually need to be done? Does the practice get more of a return on investment than the cost of achieving it?'

If not... **decide to stop doing it now!** I'm amazed at how many jobs on the list fall into this category when I first pull together a list with an accountant. Just cross them off the list.

If a job really does need to be done, you need to ask yourself, 'Who is the most effective person in my practice to carry out this task if I don't do it?' (Notice I said 'effective' there. That's not necessarily the cheapest.)

> As well as the inevitable to-do list you have, you also need a 'Stop-Doing' list.

If it's not currently you, then delegate it. If it is you, as there's no one else in the practice to do it, *you need to start training someone to take that task over from you.*

Start with the little things and move up to the bigger ones. Before you know it, you'll be doing the work you enjoy, the work that only you can do to have the most impact on your customers.

Two further points to note...

As you're delegating tasks and training people to do them, be aware of resources. Sometimes you'll know that a person has the capacity and can take them on without breaking a sweat. At other times you might need to reallocate tasks from them to someone else so they have the capacity to do the tasks you want them to do.

Secondly, ask yourself: 'Is there a number (KPI) I can measure to demonstrate I am making progress?' It could be as crude as the number of items on your Stop-Doing list and the amount they reduce each month. It could be the number of hours you save each month by stopping doing things. Have a think – it might just give you a little more focus.

## Even Longer Game: Skills Matrix

The simplicity of this tool never ceases to amaze me, but it will have a profound impact on your workload and the ability of your team members to do your work for you if you implement it thoroughly.

| |
|---|
| Download an example of a Skills Matrix and watch a quick video explanation at www.BanishTheBottleneck.com/FreeGiftsFromSimon |

Once you have downloaded the skills matrix, you'll notice there are two sheets. They both work on the same principle. The sheet entitled Pre-Advisor lists all the skills I believe a team member needs to prepare a set of accounts for review. These skills include:

- Prepare sales and purchase invoices on Xero

- Reconcile bank accounts on Xero using both bank feeds and statement imports
- Use Xero's "Find & recode" function
- Use Xero's expenses module
- Add a scanned receipt to Xero
- Use Xero's inventory stock control module
- Produce standard reports from Xero: P&L, Balance Sheet, Aged Receivables
- Produce a VAT return report in Xero and file it
- Bulk upload sales invoices to Xero
- Bulk delete invoices in Xero
- Use Xero's Knowledge Base to advise and direct clients
- Pass Xero certification
- Solve routine client Xero queries
- Train clients to use Xero
- Transfer from Sage/ QuickBooks/ FreeAgent to Xero

Add any skills you think a team member needs that are missing and remove any you feel are surplus. Don't get caught up on the software mentioned, just change it to what you use.

Similarly, the Advisor sheet contains all the competencies I believe a team member needs to be able to advise customers as their relationship manager. You will also see that the Advisor sheet is loosely grouped into six sections. The idea is that each section takes about six months to complete, although many GreenStones team members move through them more quickly. The first six months' skills include:

- Produce final accounts with a Trial Balance that reconciles
- Produce final accounts with a Trial Balance that reconciles, including tax computations
- Answer customer questions about Xero over the phone and use internet access to solve computer software

      problems remotely
- Produce accounts records checklist for completion by the customer
- Understand associated company rules
- Identify customers suitable for flat rate scheme, on those reaching limits
- Identify customers who have breached the registration threshold
- Demonstrate the ability to calculate payroll manually
- Advise and train customer using Xero's payroll
- Advise and train customer using Sage's payroll
- Prepare a reply to a professional clearance letter

Now here's how you use these documents…

On the top row of the spreadsheet, in the columns, you enter your team members' names. Then, for each skill, in the cross section, you colour code the box red, amber or green. Red is for 'not working on yet' (notice the positive spin there: I don't say 'can't do this', – I indicate that they aren't doing it *yet*!). Amber is for 'working on'. Green is for 'competent'. Then, at a glance, you can see which team member is competent at what skill and what they are working towards.

The spreadsheet should form the basis of each team member's career development review and act as a training needs analysis at the same time.

# STEP 5:
## SET THE PERSONAL KPIS

# Step 5 – Set the Personal KPIs

## Team Member KPIs

You have begun the process of empowering your team to take over much of the work that you used to pile on your own plate. But in order for them to be successful at completing their responsibilities, the team need to have their own personal KPIs.

Setting team member KPIs is a vital step in removing yourself as the bottleneck for your practice. Each team member must have a certain set of responsibilities. If they are properly trained and motivated to do them, you no longer need to micromanage how those tasks get done.

Once each KPI has been allocated, it's then up to the team member to produce those results (with your support) in return for their salary.

## The 3 Qs

Every team member needs at least three KPIs. These KPIs should be measured and recorded on the employee's PSOCK, or Personal Statement of Current KPIs.

Those three base KPIs need to be in three areas:

- Quantity
- Quality
- Qualification.

Otherwise, you end you with very little perfect work or lots of rubbish work! And your team members don't develop, either.

I should point out that not every number on the individual KPIs needs to be on the BSOCK, but it helps if team members can see how their numbers directly affect the numbers of the practice.

Let's look at the three areas in a little more detail.

## Quantity

This set of numbers is often the easiest for you to identify and implement as you have been focusing on them since the start.

They can include:

- fees produced
- invoices processed
- leads generated
- leads converted
- number of letters written
- turnaround times for parts of accounts jobs
- proactive calls made.

There's a lot – just don't get carried away with them!

## *Quality*

These KPIs tend to be a little bit more difficult to come up with and to measure. You may need to be creative in order to track them. Some practice owners use this as an excuse not to have any, but I know you won't do that.

Here are a few ideas for quality measures:

- accounts learning points
- payroll reruns (on our mistake)
- review learning points
- typing mistakes
- number of customer complaints.

You might feel the urge to add some sort of customer opinion of quality here, such as a customer survey. I'd discourage that.

In my experience, customers have a very poor grasp on 'quality'. I'm sure you've seen the same horror shows as I have when you ask for professional clearance. Up until you took over, they thought the outgoing accountant was doing a quality job!

They're just not the best judge.

## Qualification

Again, we're assuming all your team members want to develop and grow. This relates back to the Skills Matrix discussed in the previous chapter. We need to measure this development for two reasons:

First, it will give you clarity on what it is you want that team member to improve on and how they're doing against that plan. You'll have identified your goals and objectives earlier and you will need to develop the team in order to achieve them. Once *you* have clarity, you'll be able to give *them* clarity on how they're going to progress.

Secondly, when team members are targeted on developing and improving, it makes them record what they've done on their PSOCK and the BSOCK. At the end of the year, those records can be reviewed, and the team member can 'rediscover' how much progress they've made. No one can ever leave your practice saying they've never been trained!

> The more they learn, the more effective they become at producing results you have agreed on.

We often assume that people only want training to take on more responsibility and earn more money. If they do, that's great, but that's not always the case.

Many team members simply want better mastery of their roles. How can they become better at preparing accounts, tax computations or answering the phone? What can they learn to be world-class in their role?

And under this system, the more they learn, the more effective they become at producing the results you've agreed on. Magic!

There's a further benefit to your employees if you've moved away from a timesheet system.

As the team member improves, they become more effective *and* more efficient. Under a traditional system where work is tracked hourly, the supervisor would then give the team member more work to do. (They love that, right? No!) However, if team members work when they like, greater efficiency actually means that the team member may be able to spend less time working!

A win for them *and* a win for you.

## *How Many KPIs Should They Have?*

As you have seen, at least three. Probably five. Could be seven at a push. Leaders and directors generally have more.

Simply put, each team member needs the minimum number of KPIs to achieve the outputs you want. At the start, it's tempting to have too many, kind of like covering your back 'just in case'.

Resist that if you can. It breeds mistrust and creates a whole series of systems and reporting admin to get the numbers you think you want.

It's far better to measure three KPIs to start with and then adjust them as the environment and practice changes over the next six months.

## Possible Team Member KPIs

### *Everything on the BSOCK*

This is the easy bit. Everything on the business scorecard (BSOCK) needs to be allocated to someone to take ownership of and be held accountable for.

And again, once a particular task has been allocated to someone else, it is no longer your sole responsibility. The name of the game is to move any you don't want to be involved in, or don't enjoy, to someone else within the business (or, of course, outsource it).

### *A Subtotal of Everything on the BSOCK*

Next up are the 'sub numbers'.

Some of the KPIs on your BSOCK will need breaking down and allocating to individual team members. Let's look at two that most practices struggle with: turnover and turnaround times.

**Turnover**

Turnover on the BSOCK should be as per the statutory accounts. It makes it easier for everyone to understand. Sometimes, however, the cost of adjusting for WIP each month outweighs the benefit of the extra detailed information it gives you.

Turnover should be recognised on PSOCKs as it is recognised on the BSOCK. The total of the PSOCK numbers should add up to the number on the BSOCK.

This will not be possible on some occasions, and you might need to use 'notional fees' on the PSOCK. (You could also adjust this on the full accounts, if you wish, by crediting sales and debiting some other nominal account, but I don't think that's necessary if there's some sort of reconciliation.)

*Notional fees*

There are many examples where you might want to credit a team member with notional fees. The idea is to keep things fair.

Say you prepare the accounts for your long-standing mate and charge them £2,600. You've never charged them market rate (£3,200) and the politics of changing that now are just too high to bear.

And why should you? They're your mate!

But this isn't fair on your team member. Why should they suffer a loss of £600 (£3,200–£2,600) just because the work is for your mate? They shouldn't. You can credit them with a notional fee of £600 once the job has been completed. In your accounts, you can credit sales and debit 'mates' rates' if you fancy it!

Another example is where the team member undertakes training over and above their normal development activities as per the PSOCK. Say, for example, you enlist the services of The Accountants' Mastermind to deliver a brilliant team Away Day. You'll want to consider using a notional fee to ensure the team does not get penalised for spending a day out of the practice (credit sales, debit training).

It will also help you reflect on the true cost of the training you are undertaking and your return on the investment.

**Turnaround times**

The biggest mistake most practices make when allocating targets to team members is to be lazy and allocate the whole time (including the customer's!) to one individual.

They will set targets like:

- the number of days after year-end the accounts are filed at Companies House (as if most customers care!);

- the number of days from books received to accounts sent to Companies House; and

- percentage of VAT returns filed within 21 days of quarter end.

All of these are rubbish KPIs at an individual level. They only work at the practice level in certain circumstances.

As an example, let's take a deeper look at the 'number of days from books received to accounts sent to Companies House'.

There might be several steps:

1. books requested

2. books received (could be the first step if you're doing the bookkeeping)

3. books checked in

4. missing information requested from customer

5. missing information received

6. draft accounts sent to customer

7. meeting arranged

8. meeting held

9. final accounts sent to customer for signature

10. signed accounts returned

11. accounts sent to Companies House.

At GreenStones, we have 39 steps in this process but the 11 steps above are enough to make the point.

At a practice level, you can influence the time from Step 1 to Step 11. For example, if you have a customer that is rubbish at bringing in missing information in Step 5, then you can choose to stop working with them.

However, for an individual team member, this is almost impossible (unless they have the authority to decide what customers the practice works with).

You might also have a situation where the person who prepares the accounts does not hold the meeting. Again, it would be unfair to measure either individual on the results of the other person.

So, what's a better way to do it?

At GreenStones, we measure total turnaround time in days at a practice level. We exclude any time taken between Steps 4 and 5, as well as Steps 7 and 8. We can't know how long it will take the customer to bring the missing information in (although we can improve how we ask). The time between ringing the customer for an appointment (Step 7) and when they can see us (Step 8) is often dictated by work patterns, holidays, etc.

Individuals are measured on the section that they have responsibility for. Someone prepares the accounts, and someone else sees the customer. The individual who prepares the accounts will be measured on the days between Steps 5 and 6. The person who sees the customer with the accounts will be measured on the days between Steps 8 and 9.

## Others Not on the BSOCK

The final KPIs that might appear on a PSOCK are where the team member needs to focus on KPIs that are important to *them* but not necessarily to *the practice as a whole*.

Here's an example: the individuals in our customer care team (administrators) have a **delight score**. As well as making sure the customers are looked after, they also service the team by scanning documents, posts, preparing reports, etc.

The delight score is measured by a survey that's sent out to the other team members each month. The team members who aren't in the customer care team rate the individual on a scale of 1 to 10 for the service they have provided over the month. That score goes on the customer care team member's scorecard.

Another example is generating leads. At GreenStones, one person is responsible for seeing potential new customers and converting them. However, a few team members have lots of contact with customers and that contact should also create leads. They are then measured on number of leads passed. Although this number does not appear on the full business scorecard, it is a key part of that team member's job.

# Setting KPIs

Here are my top tips for making sure the one-to-ones are a success:

How are the KPIs set? It's a joint conversation, a team effort.

Now, be warned: You may have set targets before and the team member agreed to them.

However, until you've set a target where your practice's survival and team member's job depends on them, you've never really set targets.

Previously, I bet it was a, 'Yeah, okay, this is what I think they should be...' with an 'Okay,' and then off you go.

If you get the target wrong, the practice declines. Yet you can't turn round to a team member and say, 'You're not working hard enough,' if they're hitting the targets you set together.

The same is true from a team member's perspective. They can

hardly complain about being dismissed if they are not hitting the numbers you agreed. As you can see, it ups the ante.

However, that level of accountability isn't possible right away. These numbers need to be correct as quickly as possible, but in the short term you might have to suffer with them being wrong.

My advice is to sit down with each team member on a one-to-one basis and begin by explaining that you're bound to get this wrong in the first instance. This gives you and the team member the opportunity to discuss the KPIs openly and make mistakes along the way. Agree to set some targets and then review them after three months.

What you'll find is that some team members are very optimistic about what they can achieve, and others are pessimistic. After running through this process a few times, you'll find a middle ground. Then you can start to look to improve the numbers.

The best thing to do is get started and modify as you go along. Just accept that there will be mistakes and debates along the way (which is a good thing).

### Accounts Fees and Suggestions

When working with other accountancy practices, I have seen accounts fees targets for individual team members as low as 2x salary and as high as 7x.

As you've seen, there are so many variables it's impossible to arrive at a 'standard'. You have your prices, the average fee per customer, the standard of work you do, the strategy you pursue, etc.

That, to a degree, is why you can't get the targets right first time. You just don't know.

Someone pursuing a 'processing strategy' (no meetings and

churn the jobs out quickly) will have a higher target than someone with higher service levels. Neither is right or wrong.

As a guide, I suggest you start at 4x salary and work from there.

## What If They Do a Mixture of Work?

Keep it simple. The method of setting the targets remains the same. You just need to think about how you allocate the results they produce.

For example, two people work on a job. They agree the target split between them. Let's say every job has two team members to work on them: an accounts production person and a director who sees the customer with the accounts.

> " The best thing to do is get started and modify as you go along.

Either allocate the whole fee to the accounts production team member (the director should have other targets!) and up the target, or guess how much of the fee is attributable to them (say 80%) and use that for each job.

Whatever you do, just be consistent and fair.

## What Happens If the Targets Do Not Add Up to the BSOCK?

They will, in most cases. Otherwise, just change the BSOCK target.

Fees generated very often won't, though. They'll either be lower, if you don't have enough capacity in the team, or higher, if the opposite is true.

If they're lower, then you have an opportunity to reward your team members to produce the outcome, or go out and recruit someone to fill the gap.

If they're higher, then you need to get out there and win some more work or reprice the work you have!

## One-to-Ones

We've discussed that KPIs should be set in one-to-one meetings. Let's take a closer look at how those should function.

First, plan to do the meetings on one day. If you do the one-to-ones over a period of days (or, even worse, weeks), then the content will change and it will cause confusion among the team. The team members who have had the one-to-ones will talk to the team members who haven't. Those team members will then feel left out or come into their meeting with you with preconceived ideas.

Conversations are clearer when they happen as soon as possible. If you can't see the entire team on the same day, at least try to do entire departments.

### Accept the Numbers May Be Off

The numbers you set together are never going to be right to start with. Accept that. Reassure the team member of that: it's an experiment and it's okay to get them wrong.

The best thing to do is put a date in the diary for the end of the first month and the first quarter to review the numbers to make sure they're fair and achievable. At that point, you can agree the targets are right and the team member can be held accountable for them, or adjust them again if necessary.

## The Initial Meeting

Start with a thank you and ask if there are any questions that arose from the team Away Day. Then explain that you have come up with some targets for them that are probably wrong. Go on to explain that you will be reviewing them at the end of the first month and first quarter.

You also need to tell them that no disciplinary action will be taken if they miss targets in the first quarter, whilst everyone learns. Be explicit about this.

Then work through the numbers one by one and explain why each is important to you and the practice. You can also share how the target was calculated, if you like.

You can then ask the team member's opinion on whether they think the targets are too low or too high, and whether they need to be adjusted. Remember you are both on the same team. This is not combat!

Finally, thank the team member for their contribution and confirm the first review date. Job done.

Allow 30 minutes for each person. In summary:

- Set the scene
- Ask them what numbers they think should be on their PSOCK
- Suggest your numbers
- Set the numbers
- Say thank you.

## The One-Month Review

What do you talk about in the first review? Pretty much the

same as the first one-to-one, except this time you have more concrete numbers to talk about. Ask how it's going for the team member and how they feel about hitting the numbers. If they've missed the numbers, reassure them that this is okay. If they have hit all the numbers, celebrate!

Unless it's absolutely clear the numbers you're measuring are wrong, resist the temptation to change anything now. A month isn't long enough to do a proper review and, if you change them now, the three-month window will start again!

### The Three-Month Meeting

This is your chance to change anything you want to, although my advice is to proceed with caution.

Sit down with the team member and make sure everything is okay. Check in with the numbers. What have you both learned? Do any of the numbers need changing? Do any of the KPIs you measure need changing?

If they do, now's your chance to make an adjustment. Reconfirm the numbers and then share what the next steps are with the team member. If you're both happy, you're up and running: you've **set the numbers.**

If you need to make major amendments, consider running another three-month grace period so they can settle in.

## Hold People Accountable

Once you are happy your target numbers are correct, it's time to start holding your team members accountable for their results. And, unfortunately, that can sometimes mean letting people go.

This is one area you might find difficult, and it's okay if you do.

Most people don't like confrontation and tend to shy away from it. But if you don't hold people accountable for their performance, everyone will notice. And before you know it, most of them won't be hitting their numbers and anarchy will set in! At some point, accountability has to lead to letting people go.

I should point out that asking someone to leave your practice is never a black-and-white situation. Stuff happens. Kids get ill, cats die and team members just have things going on outside work that affect their performance. Only you can decide how much support you're going to give, and when enough is enough and you need to take action.

I learned this first-hand when I first introduced personal KPIs.

Everything started off okay. We hit our numbers. Profits and practice performance was up. Then, after about eight months, the numbers started going down and I soon worked out why: I wasn't holding people accountable.

One person had missed their numbers slightly and I'd brushed it off. That had led to a couple more team members missing their targets, then a couple more and a couple more.

After eight months, most weren't hitting their numbers.

I needed to hold everybody accountable to make sure the practice was safe. Eventually, it was time to let someone go.

It was embarrassing.

*I had to dismiss the same person twice in three weeks.*

It was in 2006, and it was the first time I'd sacked someone. Let's call the team member Jack. I'd been putting off getting rid of Jack for months.

I knew Jack wasn't right for us. I'd spent ages training him. I was changing systems to work around him, yet he wasn't performing anywhere near the level I needed him to.

The time had come. I sat down with him and explained for the umpteenth time what the problems were. I waffled a lot, didn't really say what I meant and tried to sugar-coat the news that was coming.

Then I told Jack I wanted him to leave and said it would be best if he went straightaway. And yet I never said the words 'you're dismissed' or 'we're letting you go'. The language I used was not so very different to the language I'd used in previous disciplinary conversations. It was not strong enough or clear enough.

I'd delayed the conversation to a late Friday afternoon so there was less disturbance for the team. Less of a long goodbye.

There were a few tears once the conversation had finished. Jack, not me. I went home, ordered pizza and opened a bottle of red wine. I also spent the whole weekend telling anyone who'd listen how horrible the entire event had been and how relieved I was that the sorry saga was now over.

*And then...*

Jack turned up to work on the Monday morning, as bold as brass. He arrived at the normal time, said hello and sat at his desk!

To begin with, I thought he'd just come in to collect some more belongings he'd forgotten to take on the Friday night.

However, I was wrong. Jack started work. He was carrying on as normal. I couldn't believe it!

Now the sad thing is, I didn't have the heart – or, more truthfully, the courage – to explain I'd sacked him on the Friday night. I just couldn't face it. I was scared.

This went on for a further *three* weeks. He'd turn up and carry on as usual. The work hadn't improved, and the situation was no better.

I am ashamed to say I only took action when I was forced to for legal reasons. Not great, I know.

This time I went armed with a letter I'd written, so Jack had absolute clarity on what I was saying. When he read it, there was a look on his face that I never want to see again. It was the sudden realisation that this was the conversation we'd had three weeks before!

I resolved never to treat a team member like that again, by deciding to be clearer and braver in my communications.

It's now 15 years later and I'm still not great at sacking people (thankfully, I've not had to do it very often) but at least I know, using the HEFFF process that follows, it has been done properly.

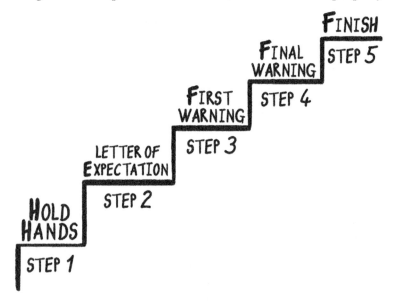

Here are some questions for you to think about...

Do you have someone in your practice who is not up to scratch? Someone you need to let go, but you are putting off making the decision? Maybe it's a customer you really should stop working with. If so, resolve right now to sort the problem out and deal with it. You are wasting so much more energy on the situation than you think.

And you will feel so much better once it's sorted. Be courageous.

## Step One: Hold Hands

The first step is to establish what's going on, if you don't already know. It's called 'hold hands', as that is how you should imagine you're working with each other at this stage. Imagine you're walking down the road together, side by side, holding hands. Working together to get to the same destination. You're playing doubles on the same side of the net, not singles on opposite sides of the net.

Have an informal conversation with the team member. Make sure you listen and see what support they need. What challenges are they currently facing, inside or outside of work? Are there skills on their Skills Matrix that they need to focus on?

Then share your concerns about their performance and what effect it's having on the team, the practice and the customers. The team member needs to understand how important it is that they hit their numbers.

Finish the conversation by agreeing on what changes are going to be made (if any) and what results you expect in the coming weeks or months. Ask them to repeat what you have said so you are both clear about what needs to happen.

## Step Two: Letter of Expectations

If the team member fails to improve their performance after the holding hands conversation, you need to go more formal.

However, as you'll see, this stage is more often a learning for the practice owner rather than the team member!

You begin by writing a letter. **You do this before you meet with the team member.**

The letter follows this format:

1. Confirm expectations – what will change and by when?

2. Confirm support and resources needed to achieve the expectations.

3. Confirm the consequence if the expectations are not met.

 Download a template for the Letter of Expectations at WWW.BANISHTHEBOTTLENECK.COM/FREEGIFTSFROMSIMON

The first part of the letter sets out your expectations of the person. It could just be the KPIs on their PSOCK, but more likely it will include other responsibilities as well. If there's a behaviour challenge, that needs to be included too.

This part of the letter also needs to confirm by what date you expect to see changes in the team member's results. The length of time will vary depending on the difficulties. You can reasonably expect the team member to sort out a behavioural problem within a week. But it will be longer if it's something like sales targets not being hit, as they can't just generate sales tomorrow if they have not been generating leads.

Next, move on to how you're going to help them resolve the

challenges you're currently facing: more training, one-on-one support, coaching, etc. What are you going to do to support the team member to achieve your expectations? You also need to consider what resources you may need to allocate to them, so they have the ability to hit the target. They might need the support from the team on a certain project or more money to buy in outside help.

Finally, you set out the consequences of what will happen if the team member fails to achieve the expectations set out in the letter. Generally, it's moving to a first warning recorded on their personnel files, but it can be anything that you have in your disciplinary procedure.

At this point, remember that you're the only person who has seen this letter. There are some important questions you can ask yourself:

- Have I given the team member this amount of clarity in my previous communication with them?

- Have I given this team member all the support and training they need to hit their numbers and carry out their duties?

- If I were the team member receiving this letter, would the comments and observations seem fair?

If you answer 'no' to any of those questions, you have work to do. You need to get clarity yourself, share that clarity with the team member, and stay at the 'holding hands' step. Over the years I've lost count of the practitioners who've gone through this process and then decided not to share the letter with the team member after all. They realised that the fault lay less with the team member and more with their own unclear expectations!

It may feel like a lot of work. You will want to revisit the letter a few times and think about it a lot before you decide you are happy with it. The first draft is always rubbish!

If you're happy with the contents of the letter and you answered 'yes' to the questions, then it's time to meet the team member again.

Set up a formal meeting to discuss the contents of the letter. Make sure you listen to what they say and take their opinions into account.

> Have I given the team member all of the support and training they need to hit their numbers and carry out their duties?

You will need to revise the letter based on that conversation. If there's additional support they've identified to help them resolve their challenges, make sure that's included in the revised letter. Once you're happy and the letter clearly sets out your expectations, the time limit for achieving them, the help and resources the team member needs to achieve them, and the consequences of not meeting expectations, then it's time to send it to them.

As I said, this may seem like a lot of work, but it pays off – and it's far less time-consuming than finding a replacement team member!

## Step Three: Formal Warning

If the team member fails to meet your expectations as per the letter, it's time to take it up a level.

All the hard work has already been done at the letter of expectations stage, so it's now just a question of reviewing the letter to see what has changed and amending it accordingly. You will want to change the consequences of failure to hit your expectations to make sure it refers to the next stage of your disciplinary procedure.

Then, meet the team member again and go through the same process as when you issued the letter of expectations.

Record the conversation and letter on the team member's personnel file.

## Step Four: Final Warning

Now we're in the last chance saloon. Simply follow the process outlined previously.

Review the letter of expectations, change it as necessary, and amend the consequences to dismissal if corrective action is not taken. You need to do this in accordance with your own disciplinary policy.

At this point, you should be asking yourself, 'Have I done everything I can for this team member?'

Being asked to leave a business should never be a surprise for a team member. If it is, you have not done your job properly in the four stages before 'finish'.

Equally, you don't want to keep delaying and delaying the inevitable. That's not good for you or them.

Since I've been operating this process, I've only ever had two team members reach this stage. Both recovered the position and went on to work for GreenStones for many more years. I have, however, had plenty who left during the three earlier stages!

## Step Five: Finish

The last stage – when they still haven't achieved your expectations – is to 'finish' them.

No business leader I have ever met likes firing team members. Some, like me, feel a failure because the recruitment or training processes have been unsuccessful. Others are just scared of the process and the reaction they might get when they hold the conversation.

If you have followed the HEFFF process up to now, then it shouldn't be a surprise to the team member.

Here are some quick tips to help you undertake this part of the process:

- Use human resources or subcontract in an expert in these matters.

- Make sure you are doing everything by the book so there is no comeback on you.

- Don't drag your feet. Make sure the process is short and smooth. Deliver your message clearly and swiftly, but with compassion. Speak in the past tense as if they have already left. It will make it more difficult to talk about 'second chances'.

- If/when the team member responds, listen to them and take their comments on board. However, do not change your mind and do not argue with them.

- Once they have left, your attention needs to turn to the team, who will want to know what happened and why, because they might think they are next! Stick to the facts and share as much as you are comfortable with. Again, it should not really come as a surprise to the team as they will have been seeing the team member's results as well. Talk about the future and what it will mean for the practice in the short term.

- Lastly, make sure you are kind to yourself. As I said at the beginning, no one likes firing people (except, perhaps, Alan Sugar). We often regret keeping someone on the team for too long but rarely regret firing someone too soon. Take a break, reflect on what you have learned, set any action you need to whilst you are in the moment to make sure you do not have to do it again, and then move on.

# Special Cases

Most of the time, team member KPIs are fairly straightforward. However, there are a number of special situations in which the numbers may not be as straightforward as discussed. Let's take a look at how to handle those situations fairly.

## Part-Time Team Members

Part-time people are treated the same as full-time people. Set their goals and then amend them as you work together to get them right.

However, you need to think about how they (or you) might deal with any time-sensitive goals like turnaround times. What happens if they work Monday to Wednesday and a job with a one-day turnaround time is passed to them on a Thursday?

It's up to you.

You can make the targets an average, change their working patterns (so they are in every day), set up a buddy system (so someone helps them out when they're not there) or take away the days they are not there from the result.

There's no hard and fast rule. Just be creative and you'll find a way. It is a lot harder, though.

## Admin Support

How do you set targets for administrative support? This question gets asked a lot and there is no brilliant answer.

Let's start with, 'Do we *need* targets for administrators?'

And the answer is... wholeheartedly, *yes!* Why not? They're part of the team and they're contributing to the performance of the practice.

Just because it's hard doesn't mean you can't do it. You need to have one from each of the three Qs. Here are some examples:

- how quickly the telephone is answered (Quantity)
- number of learning points (mistakes) in letters and emails (Quality)
- days taken to arrange meetings (Quantity)
- outstanding items on control panels (Quantity)
- development activities (Qualification).

Often the best solution is to ask the team member who's doing the role to see what they think the numbers should be. It's often an enlightening conversation for you and them!

## Odd Jobs

What about answering the phone, making drinks and all the other odd jobs that need doing? They'll still do them! Your team are all normal human beings that want to succeed. If they don't, they shouldn't be working for you.

They'll carry on making the drinks, answering the phone, changing the light bulbs, etc, as they do now!

That won't stop just because you have set clear goals for them and started measuring them on them. In fact, they should have more time to do those little things with less pressure as you have given them the efficiency that comes with clarity.

## Handling One-Off Projects

How do one-off projects fit into all this? You know, things like implementing software, writing systems and marketing. These are things that don't necessarily have KPIs where *you* usually end up doing them.

You have two choices. One is to max out every individual with their targets and then 'discount' them when you have a one-off project you need to complete.

For example, if someone is billing £10,000 a month and you want them to undertake a project which you think will take about half a month, you reduce their target for that month by £5,000.

Or you can build some slack into the system and make sure you keep adding in projects to use up that slack.

The first option has more clarity, and you can also see the true cost of any project or training you're going to undertake. It exposes the 'time' cost of doing something.

The second option saves you having to negotiate the 'discount' each time a new project that needs doing comes along.

My preference is the 'discount' as it keeps both you and the team member focused on the outcomes.

## Holidays

Depending on how your practice is structured, you can handle holidays in a couple of ways.

If you currently hold up everything that materialises whilst someone is on holiday until they get back, you can continue to do so. They just get swamped when they return and feel like they have not had a holiday at all within a couple of hours. (A bit like you do when you go away!)

The alternative is to share the work among the team members that aren't on holiday. They chip in and support the team member that is away. Each of them has a little more work to do while their colleague is away but, when that person returns, they feel like they have had a break.

If you do this and want to get pedantic about it, you can move the targets for each team member to reflect the extra work done. However, you'll find it all evens itself out over time.

# Recording Your Team-Member Numbers

How do you track all of these team-member numbers? In essence, the same way you track your business KPIs.

### Excel Sheet

You will remember there are hundreds of different systems out there to record KPIs and yet we still use Excel.

Our BSOCK is on Excel and the PSOCKs are on the same worksheet.

It works the same as the BSOCK except the KPIs are grouped by team member.

| | | Last Quarter | | | Month 12 | | |
|---|---|---|---|---|---|---|---|
| 37 | | | | | | | |
| 38 | **PSOCKS** | | | | | | |
| 39 | | | Last Quarter | | | Month 12 | |
| 40 | | Actual | Target | Difference | Actual | Target | Difference |
| 41 | Director 1 | | | | | | |
| 42 | Purpose Number | 455,000 | 450,000 | 5,000 | 145,000 | 150,000 | (5,000) |
| 43 | Team Happiness | 27.0 | 25.5 | 1.5 | 9.2 | 8.5 | 0.7 |
| 44 | Customer happiness | 27.4 | 27.0 | 0.4 | 9.2 | 9.0 | 0.2 |
| 45 | Team Costs/Fees | 154% | 126% | (28)% | 50% | 42% | (8)% |
| 46 | EWOs/Fee | 28% | 45% | (17)% | 8% | 15% | (7)% |
| 47 | Fees Invoiced | 15,500 | 15,000 | 500 | 6,500 | 5,000 | 1,500 |
| 48 | | | | | | | |
| 49 | **Team Member 1** | | | | | | |
| 50 | Fees Invoiced | 31,000 | 30,000 | 1,000 | 8,000 | 10,000 | (2,000) |
| 51 | Learning Points | 3.0 | 3.0 | 0.0 | 1.0 | 1.0 | 0.0 |
| 52 | | | | | | | |
| 53 | **Team Member 2** | | | | | | |
| 54 | Fees Invoiced | 16,000 | 18,000 | (2,000) | 4,500 | 6,000 | (1,500) |
| 55 | Learning Points | 2.0 | 1.5 | (0.5) | 0.5 | 0.5 | 0.0 |
| 56 | Leads Generated | 2 | 3 | (1) | 1 | 1 | 0 |
| 57 | | | | | | | |
| 58 | **Team Member 3** | | | | | | |
| 59 | Fees Invoiced | 23,000 | 24,000 | (1,000) | 9,000 | 8,000 | 1,000 |
| 60 | Learning Points | 7.0 | 6.0 | (1.0) | 2.5 | 2.0 | (0.5) |
| 61 | | | | | | | |

*Example of a PSOCK*

This allows you to get a summary of a team member's performance across all of the KPIs they are accountable for, at a glance.

---

Download a detailed example of
a BSOCK and PSOCK as an Excel file at
WWW.BANISHTHEBOTTLENECK.COM/FREEGIFTSFROMSIMON

---

You will also find on the above webpage a video I have prepared explaining how I would interpret the numbers in the examples shown.

## Who Puts Them on the Sheet?

The team member does! Next question: 'What about if they lie?'

If you expect they're going to lie, they shouldn't be working for you in the first place!

When a team member puts their results onto the spreadsheet (or into whatever software you choose to use) it helps them take ownership of it. It's their numbers going into the practice results. If you use a spreadsheet, as we do, then they can even see how entering the numbers affects the numbers of the practice as they move instantly.

# TSOCKs

TSOCKs stands for **Team Statement of Current KPIs**.

You'll notice we haven't talked much about teams. We have only talked about BSOCKs and PSOCKs.

It's simple. If you have teams, the PSOCKs add up to the TSOCKs, and the TSOCKs add up to the BSOCKs.

However, there's one thing you need to be very careful of. If you're going to have a TSOCK, there needs to be someone who's responsible and accountable for the team numbers. If not, what's the point of having one?

If you make a team member accountable for the numbers (in other words, they can get sacked if they're not achieved), then they also need the authority to take action. Ultimately, this means being able to hire and fire someone in the team. A team member can never be truly accountable if they don't have the authority to take action to deliver the results you have set.

You need to be comfortable with that. If you trust your team leader (and you should), then that's one more way of removing yourself as the bottleneck.

# Stick to Your Numbers

Once you've set numbers for KPIs and team-member KPIs,

you'll have an overriding desire to keep tweaking the numbers. *Don't*. Once you have them at this stage, **set** them. Stick with them for at least six months and review them then. If not, you end up having more conversations about whether you are measuring the right numbers in the right way with the right targets than talking about the results and the action you're going to take.

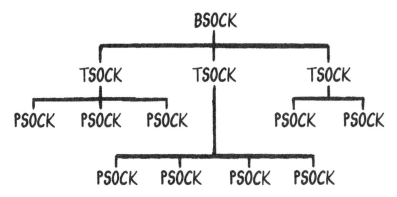

# STEP 6:
# UNITE AROUND PROGRESS

# Step 6 – Unite Around Progress

Nothing brings people together like meeting a common goal. How does your team know if they've met the goals that they helped you set at the Away Day?

You need to publish your BSOCKs and PSOCKs!

I get asked a lot if that's the right course of action, and the answer is: yes, yes and in case you missed it, *yes*!

This is just one more way of removing yourself as the bottleneck of your practice. Sharing information with the team gives them a sense of ownership in the practice. And along with that sense of ownership comes the competence and confidence to make decisions on your behalf.

## Look Forward, Not Backward

As you prepare to share your numbers, it's important to remember to focus on the current month and next month – not last month!

As accountants, we've been trained to report on history. However, it doesn't matter how much you talk about last month's or last year's numbers – you're never going to change them.

When you focus on the past internally it is all too easy to apportion blame, and the whole process becomes a negative experience for those involved.

Of course there are lessons to be learned from the past, but make sure they're in the context of how they will change the next set of numbers to be reported.

After years of training, this is harder than you think!

# Sharing the Numbers

Below are comments and questions accountants ask about publishing and sharing numbers, together with my normal responses.

## How Should I Share Them?

If you are using the combined BSOCK, TSOCK and PSOCK spreadsheet which was shared with you earlier, then that should be saved in an accessible place.

The team can then look at it any time they like and update it as their numbers change.

In the beginning, I recommend holding a monthly meeting where everyone is free to ask questions and discuss the numbers. You'll want to talk them through the numbers on the BSOCK and how they relate to the targets you shared on the Away Day. You'll also need to explain (probably more than once) how the numbers are calculated and what they mean. Once you've been sharing the numbers for a few months, you might find you no longer need to have the monthly meeting, as everyone will be looking at the numbers more regularly.

It's also a great idea to get the team members to report on their PSOCK in small groups (no more than six people). The presentation should follow a simple agenda and take no more than 30 minutes.

- What did you say you were going to do last month? Have you done it?

- What were this month's numbers?

- What are you going to do to improve next month's numbers?

Never criticise a team member in this meeting and make sure their colleagues ask clarifying questions rather than offer judgements or opinions. When you mix up the teams, you'll find everyone ends up with a better understanding of what each other is doing and it will make it easier for them to support each other.

> *It doesn't matter how much you talk about last month's or last year's numbers – you're never going to change them.*

## Who Fills the Numbers In?

The person who's responsible for the KPI does. The physical act of entering the result into the spreadsheet (or whatever software you are using) means they will be more connected to them. As they enter the KPIs they will see the practice numbers move and they will feel part of what the practice is achieving. It helps them take ownership of their numbers.

## How Do I Get My Team to Fill Them In?

You get what you tolerate. They won't fill in all the numbers to start with. You will get resistance to the extra admin, although it really doesn't take that long to do. The resistance is more to do with the system being new and that for the first time the team member's output and productivity is being 'exposed' to the other members of the team.

You need to keep chasing and encouraging them to do it. Reward the ones that do so that they keep completing them. Create a game of it if you like, and ultimately hold them accountable if they don't do it.

Completing the KPIs will become a habit very quickly. They'll also focus on the numbers you talk about the most. They'll know they are the numbers that are most important to you. They'll then focus on them as well. So be careful with your language when you're speaking to the team about the numbers. Make sure you are talking about the ones you want them to focus on too.

## What Will They Think of My Profits?

Usually, they don't care. If they wanted to, they'd have worked out roughly what your profits are before you even tell them. Very often they think you're earning more than you actually are. But, as I said, generally they don't care.

They're just numbers. If they do care, maybe they're not the right people to have in the team.

## What If I Make a Loss?

If this is a blip, just explain it as such.

But if it's more than that, as Winston Churchill said, 'Never waste a good crisis.'

If there have been a series of crises, you need to share this to reassure the team and hold on to their trust. This will keep them on board with the changes you need to make to get the practice profitable again. They might even have some ideas on how to do that.

## Who Should See the Numbers?

Everyone!

## Even My Customers?

If they're relevant to them, yes!

If you measure things like turnaround times, customer happiness, proactivity and your purpose number, they can all be shared on your website, on a board in reception and on social media too. These numbers can be great marketing material!

We accountants are numbers people, after all, and if we can't measure our numbers and share them, what hope do we have of getting our customers to do this?

# Make It a Game

There are lots of ways to make reporting and hitting the numbers a big win for the team members and the practice.

You can play games individually, as teams or as the whole practice. It's up to you. Here are a few ideas. Have fun with them!

## Fake Money

Get a graphics designer to create some notes in values that are appropriate for your practice. You'll want to be king or queen on one side, and on the other side you could put famous business owners you and the team aspire to be like.

Once you have the designs, print them out (your photocopier will do!) and cut them up. You can download a PDF of the £250 and £500 notes we created from the Free Gifts page and modify them to suit your own practice. (I bet you can't guess who the inspiration is on the £250 note!)

You can then 'issue' the notes to your team when they contribute to their targets. The easy one for this is if they have a billing target. You can give them notes each time they send an invoice out. If they bill £1,000 towards their £5,000 target, you give them £1,000 when the invoice goes out.

*The notes hanging above the team members' desk in the GreenStones office*

A more overt way of monitoring this is to pin the notes to the ceiling above the team member's head.

If their target is £5,000 for the month then pin notes to the value of £5,000 above their head. Each time they send an invoice out you take that value off the ceiling. In real time, you can see what each team member has to bill and obviously all the notes on the ceiling add up to what the practice has to bill for the rest of the month.

A slightly gentler way to introduce this concept is to start the month with a pile of notes that add up to the practice billing target for the month. Then, as each team member sends an invoice out you can remove that value from the pile of notes. It still focuses the team on the billing target (tangibility), but it is less pressured than the notes on the ceiling.

If you have a target you want to hit, like tax returns to be filed, you can use balloons instead of notes. This is an idea I first saw used at an accountancy practice in Essex called Blue Rocket. Basically, you pin the number of balloons to the ceiling representing the number of returns that still need to be filed. Each time one is filed, a balloon

> *Never waste a good crisis.*
> *— Winston Churchill*

gets popped, so you can see how many returns you have left to file. An advancement on this is to include little prizes inside some or all of the balloons, so every now and then someone gets a treat.

## Thermometer

You'll have seen these used in a lot of places to show how far an organisation has got with their fundraising efforts. Well, you can use it too.

You can buy a cardboard thermometer for a few pounds from Amazon. All you need to do is decide on your scale and then make someone responsible for colouring it in as you progress up the thermometer.

Put the thermometer somewhere everyone can see, and it becomes a visual representation of how you're doing.

You can also use the thermometer to play games and add a little fun into the office. For example, you could ban common words from the office vocabulary like 'debit', 'bank', 'records', etc. Every time someone says a banned word, they move up the scale (and pay a fine!).

## Test Tube

This is a slightly different take on the thermometer. Buy a large plastic test tube from the likes of Amazon and put a scale on the side working towards what you want to achieve.

Let's use the tax return example again.

The top of the tube becomes 'all tax returns filed'. In a separate bag you have the number of marbles that add up to the total number of tax returns you have left to file.

Each time a return gets filed, the person who filed it takes a marble out of the bag and pops it in the test tube. The test tube represents both the number of returns filed and the number left to do.

## Battleships, Wheel of Fortune, etc

You can use any board game for this one. The team might have some good ideas.

Rather than taking turns, each team member must 'earn' a turn at the game by accomplishing something. It could be filing a tax return, living by the practice values or getting a great review from a customer. You can focus and reward any behaviour you want. This changes up the typical mode of play because sometimes one team member may take several turns in a row.

When they take a turn at the game they are awarded points based on the result of that turn. For example, if you're playing Battleships, it could be five points for a direct hit, two points for a close miss and no points for a miss. After each turn you add the points scored to the team member's previous total. After a predetermined length of time (say, a month) a winner is declared.

## What Should the Prizes Be?

Cash prizes are great, but experiences and personalised gifts are far better. It's harder work to organise but the payback is so much more.

Here's a quick example of when I hit the 'reward' nail on the head by simply *listening* to what my team members were saying.

One of the joys of working in a results-centred practice is that the team members no longer feel like they need to have their heads down when you are around. If they choose to chat, it's their time they're using, not yours: they still need to 'hit their numbers'.

When they're chatting in a relaxed way, they often share things they wouldn't in a more formal environment.

On one occasion, I overheard Julie saying her GHD hair straightener had broken. Now, I'm no expert in hair straighteners (let alone the GHD variety), but a quick Google search revealed what they were, and I filed a note in my memory bank that it was something Julie wanted.

As soon as the opportunity presented itself I rewarded Julie with a GHD hair straightener. It went down brilliantly. The joke in the office was that I was the second man Julie thought about each day after her husband.

Every morning, whenever she uses the hair straightener, she (consciously or unconsciously) remembers that she is valued and listened to at work.

It's a gift that keeps on giving. You can never achieve a connection like that with cash!

# STEP 7
## PROJECT FORWARD

# Step 7 – Project Forward

Let's assume you've been running the SOCKSUP process for at least six months. You've been working with your numbers, holding your team accountable, having fun and celebrating successes. You personally have been doing less work, you are less of a bottleneck in your practice and you are delegating work instead of abdicating it.

Where now?

Here are a few things for you to consider.

## Do You Have the Right KPIs?

As you now realise, the team's output numbers are central to this process.

At an appropriate point in time (probably at the end of the first year of sharing the BSOCK) make sure you review and agree as a team what your next set of numbers should be.

Are you still measuring the right numbers for the practice?

Are you measuring the right numbers for each individual?

Are there new numbers that need adding?

Are there projects that you should be focusing on?

Are your numbers an accurate measure of where you want your practice to go?

About every six months, check that what you are measuring really helps you meet your goals. If you review them more often than that you'll risk talking *about* the numbers at the expense of working *with* them!

## Pay Rises in Return for Output?

Over the last several months, you've had some team members who have excelled and have beaten their target consistently. They might even have come to you for a pay rise already.

So, do you give them a pay rise or not?

If they are happy to deliver more output consistently, then say 'yes'!

Occasionally, you might want to ask them to prove they can excel by tracking them over the next three months before giving them a pay rise. After all, you're getting a higher return on your investment than you were when the original salary was set, so shouldn't the team member benefit from that as well?

Treat them fairly, pay them well and reap even greater rewards.

## What About Promotions?

Just as you can speak to a team member about getting a pay rise for increasing their outputs, you can also talk to them about what their future numbers need to be to get promoted.

You can project forward their numbers so they have a target to aim at.

# Another Away Day?

Yes, do it again! Round and round we go.

Set the scene and outline the plan for the next stage in the development of your practice. Celebrate the success you've had and share the vision for the coming months.

Each time you run the process your energy will increase, the team will get ever more clarity, you build more trust and that leads to more debates, more commitment and more success.

# Imagine What's Next

I want you now to imagine your practice at its best. Imagine yourself removing the roadworks from the motorway and seeing the bottleneck begin to clear. Picture it running smoothly and freely, without your constant micromanagement.

Your team members are confident, competent and committed to the practice's success. You work a reasonable number of hours each week, and then you leave to spend time with your family and pursue other passions. You trust your team to accomplish the goals you've set together even if you are not watching.

Congratulations. By reading this book, you have taken the first step towards that picture.

But if you don't take action, nothing will change.

What is the next step you need to take? What can you begin to implement *today* to bring yourself towards the future you want for your practice?

I wish you every success.

# An Invitation to You...

As you work towards that vision of a better practice and a better life, I want to be by your side.

I want to help you up when you fall over and celebrate those little wins (and big ones too!) along the way.

I invite you to join The Accountants' Mastermind, our growing community of accountants who believe there is a better way. A community of accountants who want to inspire, challenge and support themselves, their team members and, ultimately, their customers to be the best they want to be.

The wider community comes together over Facebook, WhatsApp and YouTube and is freely accessible to any owner or director of an accountancy practice. It is genuinely inspiring, challenging and supporting to be a part of it.

There are a number of ways to join. You'll find them all here…

www.TheAccountantsMastermind.com/community

I'll then be able to inspire, challenge and support *you* to be the best you want to be.

Let's get started.

## What is The Accountants' Mastermind?

Sticking wings on a bike won't make it fly!

But so many accountants do it. They see new wings (new software, social media training, outsourcing, telesales – just name the latest craze), they buy it, stick it on their 'bike', then pedal like crazy to get it to take off.

But their practice doesn't take off.

They just end up worn out from all the pedalling with a crazily heavy bike.

Masterminding is not a gadget to stick on your bike. It is a process that teaches you to dismantle your bike and reassemble it into something new.

It is about collaboration and support. It's about learning a little bit more about each other and yourself each time you meet.

Here's what we do at our Mastermind meetings:

- hold each other accountable for the actions we set
- share best practice tools, tips and tricks for running a better accountancy practice
- have world-class experts share leading edge ideas and concepts
- have a 'hot seat process'.

This last one is where the magic truly happens. In a hot seat process, one member at a time presents a problem, and we work together to get to the root of it by asking smart, clarifying questions. This process empowers you to find solutions to complex problems in your business.

Little by little, you start to see your business take off. It begins to run like a well-oiled machine. Soon, you not only have a flying bike, you have a bike that flies itself!

To join us for free and without obligation, visit www.TheAccountantsMastermind.com/community now.
We would love to see *you* grow and thrive, along with us!

# Acknowledgements

I want to thank all the people who have helped me in writing this book...

*My Grandad Garner:* He ignited my ambition to work for myself. The way he worked with his customers, his generosity and his contribution to the community are inspirational. He is the most hardworking man I know. I worked for Grandad for almost 20 years in different roles. Although I didn't see it at the time, his 'schooling' has been pivotal in my success.

*The team:* They contributed massively to the way we now work and the learnings you've read in this book. David Swann, Mark Wrigley, Sally Wrigley, Lian Stevens, Nathan Hopkins, Beverly Ingram, Julie Tuttlebee, Leigh Barraclough and Michael Weatherington were courageous enough to follow the vision and learn as we experimented with different ways of working. It has not always been a smooth ride, but it has been hugely rewarding.

*Paul Dunn:* My journey in the world of accountancy began when I read Paul's book (co-authored with Ron Baker) *The Firm of The Future*. I started reading it when I first bought GreenStones. I knew there was a better way, but not what that way was. Paul's words resonated with me so much. In 2012 Paul attended one of my presentations and the testimonial he wrote that day (which is printed at the start of this book) changed my life. I often read his words when I need encouragement. I'm not sure I'd be doing what I'm doing now without his energy behind me.

*Steve Pipe:* Steve, via AVN, gave me the tools I needed to

implement the ideas in Paul's book. His passion for the profession and his caring and loving nature have been an inspiration since the first day I met him. It was through AVN I joined my first mastermind group.

*Sanjay Shah:* Sanjay is a guiding, spiritual light in my life who started me on my journey of self-discovery. The first meeting I had with Sanjay profoundly affected my emotional intelligence and how I now coach accountants. The decision to start The Accountants' Mastermind was made in the passenger seat of his car as we drove to an event one wet Monday night in Birmingham. His support whilst my mum was dying of cancer in 2008 helped me connect more with her than I'd ever done before.

*Paul Shrimpling:* Paul played a fundamental part in the growth of GreenStones. His insight, enthusiasm, and the way he challenged me were essential to my learning. I went from being an accountant working in an accountancy practice to becoming a business owner. Paul's encouragement to allow my team to work where and when they like helped formulate my thinking. My decision to make that change was on a snowy December day in Hyde Park, London, whilst walking with Paul. Other than my wife Sally and my children Ben and Aimie, Paul is my favourite walking partner.

*Rob Walsh and Nigel Bennet:* Rob and Nigel were members of my first ever mastermind group. Another gift from Steve Pipe. Both are accountants in practice, and the support they have given me over the years has been invaluable. Although not much older than me, both have been 'accountancy father figures' helping me see sense when I'm throwing a child-like tantrum, reining in my creativity when it goes too far. Their love of their families, their teams and their customers is aspirational for me.

And special mentions go to...

Joanne Law, who has been cheering me on since the first day I met her.

Lorraine Ellison, Michael Godsmark and Nikolai Naylor, who read an early draft of this book and helped me make it better.

James Ashford and Michael Tipper, who inspired some of the models included in the book.

And, finally, Chris Payne and his team (Farah Canicosa (layout), Emily Daw (editing), Ken Leeder (cover design) and Jorge Marme (illustrations)), who have been instrumental in making sure this book is the best it can be.

Thank you all.

# Index

Printed in Great Britain
by Amazon